BOOK TWO

LOST OTTAWA

BOOK TWO

LOST
OTTAWA

DAVID McGEE

OTTAWA
PRESS AND
PUBLISHING

OTTAWA
PRESS AND
PUBLISHING

ottawapressandpublishing.com

ISBN 978-1-988437-07-1 (pbk.)
ISBN 978-1-988437-08-8 (epub)
ISBN 978-1-988437-09-5 (mobi)

Design and composition: Magdalene Carson / New Leaf Publication Design

Cataloguing in Publication data available at Library and Archives Canada

The author has made every attempt to locate the sources of photographs.
Should there be errors or omissions, please contact the author
for correction in future printings.

Contents

FALL

SECOND WINTER

Acknowledgements

Lost Ottawa is a unique form of history that requires a large number of people to create. We have many people to acknowledge!

I'd like to start by once again thanking the people at various digital repositories for making their wonderful pictures of Ottawa available online, including the Canada Science and Technology Museum, Library and Archives Canada, the Bytown Museum and especially the City of Ottawa Archives.

I'd like to thank the Ottawa Public Library for providing the superb resources of the Ottawa Room.

Next, I want to thank the staff at the Ottawa Impact Hub for providing the calm and helpful environment in which this book was written and assembled.

Special thanks to all those who have provided the extra advice and expertise needed to make Lost Ottawa a success, especially Vita Sgardello, Fred Sune, Stephanie Mitchell, and Cassandra Marsillo.

I can't let the opportunity pass by without saying thanks to Ron Corbett of Ottawa Press and Publishing for his support, and to Magdalene Carson of New Leaf Publication Design for her work on the book.

I'd like to express my deepest appreciation to the hundreds of people who have sent pictures to Lost Ottawa on Facebook over the years, and to the thousands of people who have commented on the posts ever since we got started in 2013. Without you, it just wouldn't work!

Finally, there's someone I can't thank enough. That's my wife Anne-Marie Battis, for putting up with this ridiculous obsession!

Introduction

Lost Ottawa is a Facebook community page devoted to the history of Ottawa. On this page, people post historical pictures of Ottawa and the Ottawa Valley on both sides of the Ottawa River. Sometimes those pictures capture people's fancy. When they do, the result is hundreds of likes and shares, and sometimes thousands of comments from people relating what they know.

Last year, we had a brainwave. We gathered the most popular posts from our first four years on Facebook and put them together in a book, then waited to see what happened.

Something happened, all right. *Lost Ottawa, Book One* became the most popular book in the nation's capital last year. In fact, it became the best-selling local interest book in all of Canada. People loved it, and practically everyone we met asked the same question – when is the next book coming out?

What could we do? People wanted more. So here it is, *Lost Ottawa, Book Two*.

What's inside? Well, in our first book, we published our most popular posts from 2013 through 2016. In our new book, we wanted to use as many of the most popular stories as we could since then, starting in January 2017 and continuing through March 2018.

That's not a calendar year, but it is a typical Ottawa year with all *five* seasons. First, it's winter and we're freezing to death. Spring dashes by, and we roast our way through summer. Fall arrives and the leaves turn. Then it's winter again! How did this happen? More freezing!

So we have five chapters, each containing a mix of stories from multiple seasons in a way that further reflects the Ottawa experience. It's winter? All we can think of is summer. Nice pictures of beaches, camping and *warmth* are very welcome. Is it summer? Then we start complaining it's darn too hot and need some pictures of hockey rinks and snow-covered streets to cool us down. All of which is to say that *Lost Ottawa, Book Two* has the same mix of stories as *Book One*. A story on practically any topic can follow a story on any other. Surprise is the name of the game!

The stories in the book aren't completely random, however. They're the most popular stories from the Facebook site as determined by the number of likes, and shares, and comments that people gave them. It just wouldn't be Lost Ottawa if people didn't have things to say about the Capitol Theatre, the Exhibition, malts at Freiman's, or that refreshing Pure Spring Ginger Ale. Every time we post on those topics we get a great response.

Nevertheless, every year is different, depending on new caches of pictures we came across, or new themes that people find interesting. For example, we posted a series of aerial shots of the suburbs that people really liked. So you'll find several aerials in this book, featuring suburban neighbourhoods and plazas like Bayshore, Carlingwood and Shoppers City West. We found another cache of pictures of corner stores, which led to a general theme about shopping, so you'll find quite a few stories about stores. Schools were a popular theme over the past 18 months, dining out was also popular, and people also had a lot to say about quite a number of drinking establishments.

You'll find 75 stories on these topics and more in *Lost Ottawa, Book Two*. As with our first book, each tale consists of a photograph, a short blurb, and an edited version of the dozens and dozens of comments that people made on the original post. We've arranged the selected comments into the form of a conversation. We've corrected them for spelling, grammar, and sometimes syntax, just to keep the conversation flowing.

Other than that, what you find in *Lost Ottawa, Book Two* is what people themselves had to say about the stories that they thought were most important, saying things that will make you laugh and sometimes sigh with recognition, telling you things you could never learn any other way.

That's what makes *Lost Ottawa, Book Two* a unique form of history. It's the history of the city told by the citizens themselves on the topics that matter to them. We hope you enjoy it!

WINTER

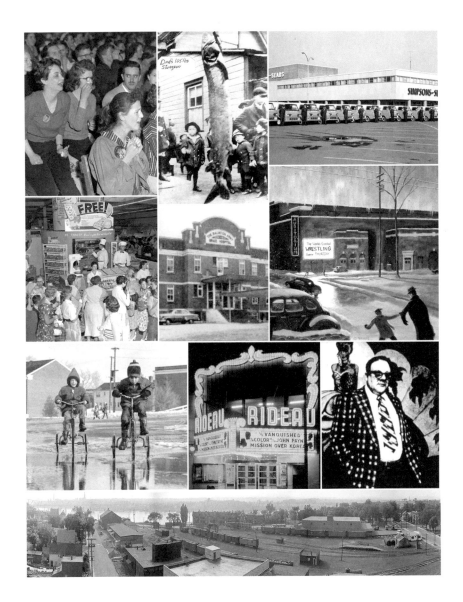

Elvis in Ottawa

The King WAS in the building on April 3, 1957. That's when Elvis played downtown Ottawa at the old Auditorium, located on the east side of O'Connor between Argyle and Catherine.

Those who were at the show remember it as if it were yesterday. Few, however, recall hearing Elvis actually sing – because there was too much screaming. Those who didn't make it to the show, well ... they seem to recall those nuns could be mean!

This post appeared on Elvis's 80th Birthday. Posthumous birthday – if you are one of those people who believe the King is actually dead.

Joe: Here's a trivia fact for you. Ottawa was one of only three places outside the United States that Elvis ever played. The others were Toronto and Vancouver.

Andrew: I didn't know Elvis even came to Ottawa. Pretty cool!

Madison: I love Elvis and I did not know about this!

Ian: I work at the hotel where he stayed. It's now called Capital Hill Hotel and Suites. Back then it was the Beacon Arms.

RB: Ah, the "Broken Arms."

Bill: My dad shared an elevator ride with the King!

Margaret: I remember the furor. I was almost eight years old and had first heard about him at a girlfriend's house. Her older sister wanted to go, but we lived in Cumberland and there was no way her parents would let her skip a full day of school to take the Voyageur bus into Ottawa on her own, and they certainly weren't going to take her!

Sean: There's a famous picture from the front page of the *Ottawa Journal* or *Citizen* of the time, featuring a 14-year-old girl who is so excited to see Elvis that she is hysterical. The girl's name was Beverly. She had skipped class to see the show (they were matinee shows back then) and got in big trouble with her father. I know her personally and can now only laugh when I think about how times have changed!

Nancy: I remember the story of a couple of Catholic girls residing at the nun's academy on Sussex who went to the concert and were expelled.

Claudette: I remember the nuns talking about the Elvis concert and telling everyone not to go, but my babysitter did. She was 16 or so, but I was only nine. My parents said I was too young.

(City of Ottawa Archives CA022970)

Eveline: I went to Catholic school and we were told we'd be thrown out of school if we attended!

Mo: Back when you feared your elders.

Eveline: No, not elders — nuns! All the teachers in our school were nuns, including the principal. It was SINFUL to go!

Isabel: I saw many great shows at the Aud ... but was a bit too young for Elvis.

Chico: I was there, playing hooky from school.

Christine: I was very young, but sat front row center with my grandmother.

Lois: I was there as a present for my ninth birthday. My mother and godmother took my sisters and I, along with two best friends. My mother and godmother wore hats, fur stoles and gloves! Crazy!

Judy: Crazy, but fun!

Carol: I was 15. What a night! Something I'll keep in my memory book for sure, but I don't think we heard any singing.

Donna: We couldn't hear him sing, it was that loud.

Fraser: Amazing to hear the screams.

Beverley: I was up in the nosebleed section at age 13. I couldn't really see him at that distance and couldn't hear him either for the screaming. But I can still say I was there!

The Rideau Theatre

Here's the marquee of the Rideau Theatre at Rideau and Dalhousie in 1953, back when people were prosperous, nobody had a TV, and the movie business was booming. Two decades later everyone had a TV, the suburban malls were calling, the local department stores were closing. Throw in the demolition of so much of the area to make way for the Rideau Centre, not to mention the building of cinemas in the new mall — and the old Rideau Theatre was doomed. It closed in 1982.

Anna: Love that marquee!

Armand: Imagine the hydro bill today!

Brian: From an era in which movie theatres were truly movie palaces.

Glenn: When I was a kid and movie theatres were a major attraction in downtown Ottawa, with their glitzy lights and lines of people waiting to go in.

Michael: This photo is so nostalgic I almost feel like I entered a time warp! Living on Daly Street in the 1950s, I saw many, many movies at the Rideau and Nelson theatres.

Marian: As well as the Capitol, Regent and Centre, when my dad would take us for a movie and a dinner on Friday nights ... until I wouldn't be caught dead out with my PARENTS on a Friday night!

Diane: I used to go to the Rideau at age nine and stay all day on Saturdays. My father would drop me off with a lunch and some spending money, too. It really was Saturday at the Movies!

Real: We would go on Saturday morning and watch three movies for 25 cents.

Bernard: Four movies for 25 cents in my day, when I remember seeing the very first James Bond movie at the Rideau. *Dr. No.* The popcorn was so good, and there was an old lady who went up and down the aisle selling treats.

Marty: I also loved the Saturday matinees, where my buddies and I went to watch James Bond (Connery), Matt Helm (Dean Martin), James Coburn and all them cool dudes. Then ... it was across the street for a malted milk at Freiman's.

Chris: Bond, Helm, Tarzan, horror, late-night marathons. A perfect day if you finished with a Freiman's malt. The original brain freeze. Got me every time!

Jacqueline: My family went to see *Monster from the Black Lagoon*, but I still don't know what the movie was about. Spent the whole movie with my face hidden behind my father's homburg hat!

Gavin: I once saw *Godzilla vs. The Smog Monster* at the Rideau. Worst movie of my life. Ran out of plot 14 minutes in. Everybody got up to leave at least four times on suspicion the smog monster was dead, but the bugger kept coming back to life!

Michael: Saw *A Hard Day's Night* there when I was a young kid.

Louise: With girls screaming as if they were at a concert.

Judy: It is amazing, when you think about how different it was back then, lining up on Rideau Street outside the theatre all night, waiting for the theatre to open, paying once and staying the entire day. And we certainly did scream!

Michael: Wasn't that such a unique time in history? When a band could have that effect on people?

Sue: I loved going to that theatre and remember all the Doris Day and Sandra Dee movies I saw there. We moved to Glabar Park when I was ten, but I had the perfect childhood in Lower Town.

Rhonda: I remember going to see Disney movies at the Rideau, many moons ago.

Dan: I recall the last years of the theatre when they alternated Disney ... with porn!

Gerry Barber of the Chaud

Gerry Barber, bouncer at the Chaudière Club along the Aylmer Road, and one of Ottawa and Hull's most notorious characters. Pictured here in a newspaper article from March of 1978.

Those of you who frequented the "Chaud" know who he was. Those of you who didn't ... might be glad you never met him!

Monique: Friday night to the disco. Saturday to the British. Sunday to the Chaud. Those were the days of my youth.

Tom: Sunday night at the Chaud. Politically, this place could not exist today, but it was an interesting place in its heyday. How many people got turfed out the front door and down the stairs and lived to talk about it? Beer in quarts. Cigarette smoke so thick. And if your life was too boring, enter the downstairs bar ...

Paul: The Chaud and Gerry Barber! Been there. Done that. Lived to talk about it! He was one scary dude to an 18-year-old.

Jay: My mother worked at the Chaud as a hostess because she was too young to serve alcohol. She told me many tales of Gerry Barber tossing the unruly out the front door without opening it first!

Robert: Oh, my. Hull in the days when the drinking age was pretty much non-existent and Gerry was a legend (and at 280 pounds he deserved it). The only times I ever saw Gerry show any fear was once with a football player who was a very big black guy trying out for the Rough Riders who was able to crush a beer glass in one hand, and another time with a little guy standing on a table with a gun. Sons used to come back to finish fights Gerry had with their fathers. All this and he served beer, too. Where has the time gone?

Arthur: I witnessed a few of those fights, and remember the one with the Rough Rider. It was my drinking hole, great action place !

Daniel: Used to see Gerry every Wednesday and Sunday at the Chaud — no cover charge nights. Saw him bounce lots of guys. I was there the night he was stabbed and another time someone took a shot. He grabbed me by the neck once for slamming my bottle on the table, which is what we all did for encores. Told me after he was not worried and I was a good kid. Phew!

Real: I knew Gerry. When he asked you to leave the building you'd better obey or else, but he was a nice guy.

Debi: Gerry was always nice to me. He once asked if I wanted to have him toss out a guy who was being a "pest." Sigh. The good ol' days.

Maureen: He let me in on a 42-year-old male's hunting license when I was a petite 16-year-old female. Spent Sunday nights there for the next three years until I left for university.

Mike: I always said, "Good evening, Mr. Barber," when I saw him at the door. His reply

(Montreal Gazette)

was always, "Hey, kid." I must have been lucky because I never saw him bounce anyone and I never did anything that would cause me to endure the wrath of Mr. Barber!

Arthur: Gerry Barber gave me a few bloody noses at the Chaud. It was a place that toughened you up, but a fun place to be!

Stephen: I feel sorry for kids today who have to sit at home and play silly games on their phones, never experiencing the real world, never having any fun. My generation was the last. God bless Gerry Barber for guiding us to adulthood. That man was a saint.

The Hayloft

Here's the Hayloft Sirloin Pit and Tavern, circa 1980, located on the northeast corner of Rideau and Waller. This was the place with the peanut shells all over the floor and famous, people say, for its "beer cheese" dip.

The Hayloft opened in 1972 and lasted into 1993. The site has been built over with condos since then. The only reminder of the block's past food glory is one lone Starbucks.

Ted: I remember this place. The funny thing is, that looks like my car parked on the street!

Geoff: Record Runner is just visible on the left. Norris Shoe Repair moved to Dalhousie in 1982. I ran the Video Station in that building until 1989.

Jambon: Too bad there isn't more of the Record Runner. My wife's father (and my wife, for a short spell) worked there from the late 1970s until the doors closed.

Hochberg: Centre du Son, Granada TV. Lots of "lost" there, including the whole building!

Mats: I worked at the Hayloft for a few weeks. Made it through training for the one-handed carry of a bus-tray around the restaurant with salt and pepper shakers with no spilling. Grill cook was a draft dodger, grouchy as hell. I remember having to make the whipped jack cheese dip for the bar. Tough job. Got fired when they found out I was 17 and underage. Made enough to buy my first stereo. Technics. Bose speakers were stolen by bikers.

Ian: I worked at the Hayloft for ten years, whenever I was in Ottawa. Being a bartender/waiter there was an incredibly important part of who I am, and who my great friends are — and a source of some of the most ridiculous memories. Hats off to the Hayloft!

Stephen: I was there on opening night. Loved it, and went regularly.

Terry: Used to go there on Saturday to nurse a hangover with French onion soup and a beer, shell some peanuts. It was the thing to do ...

Liz: In Ontario you had to eat on Sundays if you wanted to drink. Onion soup for everyone!

Tim: French onion soup and peanuts in the shell.

Tom: Oh my GAWD. Sitting in that place drinking, eating peanuts, and just watching the world go by ... a lovely Sunday afternoon.

Louis: Spent many a Friday afternoon there in my university days. Peanuts, and that amazing cheddar spread.

Cindy: The Hayloft was our go-to birthday dinner spot.

Nick: It's the only place I was ever asked to leave!

Lindsay: I remember going to the Hayloft for dinner and looking over an indoor swimming pool while there ... unless I'm crazy?

Geoff: Crazy. No pool.

Sue: Gosh, I'm sure there was another Hayloft on Lancaster, where one side of the restaurant was completely glassed in, overlooking the pool.

Helene: One Hayloft. No pool.

Ess: Two Haylofts. Second one on Lancaster at the Ottawa Athletic Association and not open as long or as popular as Rideau.

Lindsay: Hooray for not being crazy!

Jacquie: The Hayloft was a great night out, back when going out for dinner and drinks was truly an event. Good old-fashioned social time. No cell phones. No internet.

Ivo: But if you happened to be wearing a tie (not that unusual in the 1970s and '80s), the waiters had a nasty habit of cutting it off. Good thing I wore cheap ties!

Stephen: They did that at IP Looney's. Hayloft, too?

Dorothy: They did it at the Hayloft in 1977 or so. I had just been married. The night I went with my new husband, the staff sang "Happy Vasectomy to You" to a man at a nearby table, then cut his tie off with a pair of oversized scissors. He looked absolutely mortified. His wife had the biggest smile.

(Shared by Curtis Webster)

The Old Auditorium

From the day it opened in 1923, to the day it was demolished in 1967, the Auditorium held a special place in the cultural life of the city.

As noted in our story about Elvis, the "Aud" was located on the corner of Argyle and O'Connor in a building that stretched all the way down to Catherine (now the site of the YMCA). In its heyday, this building was sort of like the Civic Centre, the Senators arena, and the National Arts Centre all rolled into one, where you could see everything from ice hockey to wrestling, and ice follies to rock n' roll.

Shared by artist Dave Rheaume, this painting of a young lad dragging his father to the Aud really captured the spirit of the place.

Jennifer: My dad took us to see the wrestling there!

Garry: My father took me there for a wrestling match with Whipper Billy Watson and Gene Kiniski when I was six years old.

Dwight: I used to play hockey there in the old Cradle Hockey League.

Cheryl: My grandfather Bill Addy was a co-founder of the Cradle Hockey League at the Aud, with Ev Tremblay. He took his two granddaughters (including me!) everywhere with him, so I spent a lot of time at the Aud as a kid. I got a puck in the mouth one time, made me wary of pucks for the rest of my life.

Timothy: I was honoured to have played hockey there as a kid in the old Cradle League. Scoring a goal was an extra thrill because your name was announced over the PA and sounded so cool in this cavernous "barn."

Arthur: I also played hockey at the Aud. Lived a block away on Park Avenue and used to collect broken sticks for Mr. Purcell, who would fix them up like new and give them to under-privileged kids who couldn't afford one.

Max: Jack Purcell — the "stick doctor." He has that park named after him on Elgin Street.

Tom: My dad played hockey at the Aud, my sister took figure-skating there, and we saw some great concerts. It was almost like a second home.

Diane: Highlight of the week was to go to see hockey games with my dad.

Robert: Remember going to see hockey games with my uncle Conrad.

Jamie: Saw the Ottawa-Hull Canadiens of the old CPHL play there.

Bernard: Saw good hockey games, and would sometimes chat with the crew of CFRA.

(Dave Rheaume)

Guy: Saw a lacrosse game there, played by a team from Hull against the Montreal Canadiens with Jacques Plante in nets!

Judy: My dad took us to see the circus at the Aud in the early 1960s.

Bobby: Went to see lots of wrestling. Also the Ottawa-Hull Canadiens ... and ELVIS!

Elaine: That's where I saw Elvis Presley, many, many years ago.

Guy: My uncle Romeo Morrissette was a police officer who met Elvis while working that day.

Elizabeth: Elvis playing in his gold suit.

Isabel: I saw so, so, many great shows there. The Stones, Gene Pitney, The Beach Boys, Bob Dylan ...

Sue: I snuck out of the house to see Bob Dylan. Climbed the big wooden gate to get in ... bad girl!

Jane: My goodness, what my sis' got away with! I didn't know ...

Sue: Oh yeah? How about the time I was sneaking out the back door and you were sneaking in?

Dave (the artist): And that's why I love painting these scenes ... to bring back all these wonderful memories! Thanks for the commentary!

Bayshore from the Air

Bayshore before the mall in this aerial, looking down on the extreme west end of Ottawa in 1964. You can see how the Queensway ended at Richmond Road, leaving an unused strip to nowhere that was used for drag racing, or so I'm told. I never saw it myself because my neighbourhood, on the other side of the not-quite-a-cloverleaf, was still a cow pasture!

Bram: I can attest to the drag races. Brand new 1964-1/2 Mustangs going at it ... complete with a flagman.

Tom: Drag racing, then Harvey's REAL hamburgers, with REAL fries that they peeled and chopped right there, and fantastic milkshakes. All there, back in the day.

Christian: I can remember the Queensway ending at March Road in the mid-1970s, with a large sign from Pitts Construction saying as much.

Geoff: I lived in one of the Bayshore Towers in 1977 and remember the Queensway was still just a two-lane highway for the run to distant Kanata.

(City of Ottawa Archives CA008841)

Donna: Moved to Crystal Beach in 1963. No buses for the first couple years because they stopped at the top of Britannia Hill and later at Bayshore.

Marlene: Moved to Crystal Beach in 1968. No buses then either. We had to take the Colonial bus downtown, but we're still in Crystal Beach. Love it!

Mike: I remember in the late 1960s, the kids would all get off the bus as it turned into Bayshore, then hitchhike to Crystal Beach. Friday night at Jack's garage there were often two or three groups of kids hitching at the same time.

Bob: My family moved to Bayshore in 1964. I can see where our townhouse was, and also see the Bayshore Country Clubhouse, where the Bayshore Mall is now. Many fond memories of times spent around the pool.

Gail: Moved from Montreal in 1966 and lived in the Downsview Apartments. There was almost nothing there then. Everyone went to Carlingwood for just about everything.

Marnie: I lived there from 1967 to 1969, when there was only a big grocery store and one bank. We also went to Carlingwood to do our shopping — but there was a drive-in and two schools!

Steven: We moved to Bayshore on December 17th, 1967. There were two rows of six garden homes each and we were the second family to move in. I really liked the Bayshore Country Club, with its indoor and outdoor pools, and gyms where I played a lot of floor hockey. We stayed until 1975. I think the four-bedroom garden home was $248 a month back then.

Mike: Before the big mall was built, I remember the little strip mall with the grocery store. Not sure which one, but in the winter of 1967-68 I got my first full-time job there as a grocery packer!

Randy: The grocery store at the original strip mall was a Steinberg's.

Steven: And the Dairy Bar attached to the Steinberg's was awesome! I got my baseball cards there.

Harry: I got my hair cut at the barber in that strip mall.

Caren: My parents lived in the apartment building across the street during the construction of Bayshore Mall. My mother always told me stories of the massive hole in the ground.

Karen: I believe a few parents worried about their kids' safety because of all the traffic that would be generated by the new mall, so they went out and removed the survey stakes.

Max: Well, that didn't work!

When Carlingwood Was New

Aerials were very popular on Lost Ottawa in the winter of 2017. Here's another one, looking north over the Carlingwood Shopping Centre in 1959, when the advance of civilization (in the form of shopping malls) had just reached Woodroffe Avenue.

Dave: They paved paradise?

Fraser: That's the old Honeywell Farm in the centre of the picture, once farmed by Ed and Fred Honeywell. When I moved to Ottawa in 1952, I used to play in the Honeywell's fields.

Cathy: I remember walking past the Honeywell farm on my way to school ... I was afraid of their bull!

Vern: What is now Fairlawn Plaza was once a farm owned by a descendant of Ira Honeywell. Barbara Helen "Nellie" Honeywell was the sister of my grandfather R.W. (Bill) Winthrop, who lived at the Olde Forge in Britannia.

Andrew: It's funny how circumscribed our lives were in 1961 when we weren't even allowed to cross Carling Avenue. In general, there was more development the nearer you were to the river, and I suppose that, further west past Woodroffe, old man Fox still had his farm.

Vern: South of Carling, Woodroffe wasn't much more than mud ruts at the time of this photo, and in the early 1950s you couldn't even drive from Woodroffe to Pinecrest along Baseline. The road was passable eastward from Pinecrest only to the McEwan farm, where Barbara Ann Scott Arena is now.

Eric: Wouldn't this have been the perfect time to realign the Woodroffe/ Carling intersection, given all the open space they had? Like they did at Baseline?

Philip: By 1959, Woodroffe South and Carling were both developing. Maybe ten years earlier they could have connected the two.

Max: I'm trying to think of all the stores they've had in Carlingwood over the years.

Steven: From Simpsons-Sears over ... Laura Secord, Fairweathers/Tip Top Tailors, Zellers, CIBC, Carlingwood Restaurant, Kiddie Kobbler, Tamblyn/ Boots/Rexall, Hallmark, Woolworths, Reitmans, RBC, Dominion ...

Bill: The Hallmark Store was and still is the Davis Agency — one of the few remaining original tenants, and to this day still Ottawa-owned!

Ellen: All our shoes were bought at Kiddy Kobbler.

Bob: Warren's Men's Wear and E.R. Fisher. Tip Top came along years later. There was Zellers and Woolworths and Bata Shoes, as well as Agnew Surpass, Canadian Imperial Bank of Commerce, Armstrong and Richardson, Bank of Nova Scotia, and the barber shop. That's what jumps out of my memory bin.

Cathy: Singer was also in that mall. My dad used to sell their sewing machines and set them up in people's homes. I always loved going to that covered outdoor mall. It seemed huge when I was a little one, and very cold some days when you walked end-to-end.

Peter: Wasn't there a record store?

Michael: At the far end of the mall, called Treble Clef.

Patricia: I remember that store! You could pick out a 45, then go into a soundproof booth and listen before you bought it. Ask your kids what a 45 is, today! Or a record player, for that matter. Then again, vinyl is coming back …

Gail: My dad would bring us kids to the Carlingwood Restaurant and talk the owner's ear off.

Michael: Just across from the restaurant was the Vic Tanny's health club down in the basement.

Dawn: Before Vic Tanny's, it was a bowling alley.

Ronald: I worked in the downstairs bowling alley (and pool hall) as a pin boy, making 25 cents per game for both five- and ten-pin. Nothing automated. All by hand.

Patricia: My dad went to Vic Tanny's for the sauna. That was his "work out."

Roni: My grandfather worked at the Vic Tanny's. He had the "Lifetime Membership" — which I guess he outlived when it folded!

The Chateau Lafayette

The Chateau Lafayette in the Byward Market, circa 1970. Sometime in the 1950s or '60s it got that awful angel stone on the facade, although it still had the traditional entrances for "Men," as well as "Ladies and Escorts."

The "Laff" is so old, people say citizens took shelter there during the Stoney Monday riots of 1849.

Dave: Ottawa is full of institutions. The Parliament Buildings, the Chateau Laurier ... and the Lafayette.

Mike: This is the one I was told to stay away from by my friends in the 1970s!

Michael: Yes, and that's also why we went there.

Louise: The charm of going to the Laff as a student was hanging out with the bad boys.

Barb: And the 25-cent draft.

Paul: Got thrown out for starting a food fight. Standing in the street shouting, "I've been thrown out of better places than this!" But they let me back in the next time. Didn't hold a grudge at all. And their pickled eggs ...

Sue: I don't think I'd ever even had a pickled egg before those days ... or since! Must make a batch!

Liz: Covered the table with 25-cent draft. Gorged on pickled eggs and grilled cheese supremes. Gerry was the waiter on the men's side, and wore one of those metal change-makers on his belt. Ah, the days of skipping classes at Lisgar ...

Darren: I was christened at the Laff at age 17, but my greatest memory is of Gerry, who was a baseball enthusiast who saw me pitching at Strathcona Park in Sandy Hill one day and asked me if I would play for a Tier 1 baseball team in Ottawa. He said I can't pay you, but free beers are a way of exchanging services. I kindly accepted. For two years, and twice a week in the summer, I closed this place. Never bought a beer, but I gladly tipped well!

Jacob: I remember drinking in there when I was only 17. Of course the bartender knew, and he looks at me and says "how about a li'l tip for the bartender." How rude of me! Got schooled ...

Shawn: My grandfather Herb Currell used to own the Laff back in the 1970s. I was only a boy, but he would bring me there on Sundays while the bar was closed to complete his paperwork and inventory. He would listen to his favourite songs on the jukebox, while I played pool and ate the pickled eggs.

I still drop in for the odd quart, just to visit memory lane.

Tania: My grandparents used to sell chickens in the market and they would have a drink there. My mom has such fond memories that we would have a pitcher or two at the Laff on her birthday. People who don't have an attachment to the place think it's a dive, but my mom and I loved the cozy, down-to-earth atmosphere. I hope I don't see it disappear during my lifetime.

Chris W: Isn't it all fancy-pants and upscale now?

Roland: But what a dive the Lafayette was then! Makes me laugh just thinking about it.

(*Lower Town Ottawa*, NCC)

Chris F: I waited tables and cleaned up at the Laff for a couple of years when I was young, 1978 to '81. I learned a lot about people ... quickly! It's an experience I wouldn't trade for anything.

Bruce: The place had so much character, including the decor, but mostly the clientele. I remember the juke box, and the controversial decision to go to CDs. Long live the Laff!

Laurie: My husband took me to the Laff for our first date bar-hopping.

Rick: Classy!

Laurie: Hey, we're still married 37 years later.

The Pure Food Building at the Ex

February 25, 2017: 143 likes, 35 shares, 27 comments, 13,773 reached

Inside the Food Building at the Ottawa Ex in 1955, where a huge crowd is sampling the goods from the Ottawa-Hull Bakery.

If it's one thing people remember about the Ex, it's the food, and it's absolutely amazing how many folks remember exactly what they ate where, whether it was inside the Food Building or at the booths of service clubs and churches outside.

Check out the kid on the right, licking his fingers after sampling the donuts. Perfect.

David: The Pure Food Building was a favourite spot!

Susan: It was the best. So busy, so exciting, so fun.

Teresa: I used to go every year with my grandmother. You'd definitely get a lot of free samples!

Ellie: So many free samples, but for me I can't forget the Lions Club ham-on-a-bun.

Janet: My dad used to take us to the Ex and especially the Pure Food Building, but my favourite was Whyte's back-bacon-on-a-bun (could eat several). That was in the 1950s and '60s.

Erin: My husband and his family always helped the Kiwanis and Kinettes with their meat-on-a-bun.

John: Peameal-bacon-on-a-bun! Yum!

Ruth: I always looked forward to the Ex. Donuts, candy apples and candy floss. Loved going into the Food Building for the goodies. My favourites were the Tiny Tom donuts, made so hot and fresh ...

Norris: It almost looks like they have Tiny Tom donuts there. Maybe their first year?

Susan: I loved those itty-bitty donuts!

Michael: Yup, pure mini-donuts with the oil still on 'em ...

Erin: Used to be if you bought 12 donuts, they would add one extra for free!

Wilhelm: The Ex was the only place you could get tacos in Ottawa back then — and only once a year.

Michael: I think the Pure Food Building was the best of the Ottawa Ex.

Terry: The loss of the Food Building marked the beginning of the end for the Ex.

Adrian: It was a rundown eyesore by my time.

Steve: Well, the city took over management, then tore down just about everything when it fell apart due to lack of maintenance. Went from maybe thirteen buildings down to about four when the TD Place renovation started. We barely saved the Aberdeen Pavilion.

Max: Heritage Ottawa waged an epic campaign in the early 1990s.

Robert: We lost so much when they abandoned the Ex.

Shirley: Back then was the best time to be a kid. At the time of this picture, you could go to the Ex at age ten without adult supervision and you never worried about being bothered by anyone.

Mike: When we lived on Gilmour, off Bank, mom would give us a quarter and we would spend the whole day at Lansdowne.

Shirley: I remember paying admission of maybe fifty cents or a dollar, and always coming home with shopping bags full of book covers and rulers, etc.

André: I notice people were so well dressed back then ... even for a fair.

Leslie: It makes me want to travel back in time.

Max: Back to the Food Building for the free samples? I'm in! And maybe I could also win that brand new dream home for a dollar ...

Lower Town Panorama

In 2017 we started to experiment with zoomable, 180-degree panoramas that people could use to pan around a scene and zoom in on the details. One of our first panoramas was this shot of the Canadian Pacific train-yard that used to cut across Lower Town from the Rideau River to Sussex Street.

The tracks were removed in 1966 and the land re-used for various embassies, apartment buildings and the Lester B. Pearson Building, but this unusual view from the 1940s brought back a trainload of memories!

Bob: FANTASTIC! This is the neighbourhood where I grew up.

Jane: I love the clothes on the line!

Lawrence: I think the clotheslines are my favourite part!

Stan: When the freight train would blow its whistle for the nearby crossing, my mum would run outside and gather the clothes off the line so they wouldn't get covered in coal smoke from the steam engine!

Paul: I was also raised in this neighbourhood and I'm thinking the pic was probably taken from the roof of the Florence Paper Company. I lived at 122 Dalhousie, then moved to 134 Cathcart Street, and trespassed on the Florence Paper property from 1946 to 1960.

Alice: I also played in the Florence yard. If we were very quiet, and stayed very still, we could see rats underneath the papers! We would yell and try as fast as possible to go up that tall fence there! What memories ... 1959!

Paul: Our house at 122 Dalhousie was part of row housing owned by Florence Paper. The train-yard was my playground, and I used to play on the huge sand

hill next to the cement mixing company (and risk being sucked down the chute). I used to sit and watch the locomotives move cars to and from Ritchie Feed and Seed, as well as Gamble-Robinson at Baird and Dalhousie Streets. Sometimes we walked the tracks on the train trestle over the Rideau River and went to the Flat Rocks swimming pools.

Tom: I showed this to my mother and it brought back lots of memories for her. She lived at 89 Dalhousie, in the row houses across from the cement plant. First brick house was Graziadei, then Rodier, then Normand (the little opening into the back yard), then Legros, and last was Robillard. Mom spoke of playing in the mud from the cement plant, swimming from the bridge ... and also the rats!

Paul: There was a lot of swimming off the train bridge over the Rideau River, but not for me. Couldn't swim! On the other hand, some of those rats made it into my house. My dad killed them with a shovel.

Cliff: My parents would have been ages seven and nine when this photo was taken. My mother lived on Bruyere Street near Dalhousie. My father's home was on Redpath, underneath what is now the Lester B. Pearson Building.

Robert: I remember these tracks from my younger days. Fruits and vegetables were picked up at that freight yard, and we used to skate at Bingham Park.

Ted: Those train tracks are a pretty brutal intrusion into an otherwise residential neighbourhood. When folks sentimentalize over rail, they're usually talking about passenger travel. We need to remember that most rail traffic was freight and rail was ugly, noisy and unromantic.

Colleen: No, no! The sounds of the rail could be as rhythmic as a pendulum clock. The whistle of the train was a signal of civilization. I loved the sound of the trains. They helped me sleep. They were like a bedtime story.

Hugh: No such thing as an unromantic train. Ever! Love the smell, love the noise!

(Library and Archives Canada 4511680-685)

The House on the Corner

Another of our experimental panoramas for 2017 featured this Queen Anne house, with its outstanding turret, located on the northwest corner of Rideau and Chapel Streets. Still there when this picture was taken in 1968, the house was eventually demolished and replaced with an apartment block.

You might think there are a lot of kids on the street, but York Street Public School was only a block away. A person once told me that there was a girls' entrance and a boys' entrance back in the day. Girls walked down one street and the boys down another, but the worst and most embarrassing thing was … the principal's office was in the girls' part of the school.

Orla: Holy cow! I remember these houses! A friend of mine who later became the first-ever female letter carrier for the post office lived in the one to the left of the turret.

Beverly: Beautiful house! Love the turret!

Susan: My grandmother lived there for years.

Dianne: It must have been very grand in its day.

Paula: All beautiful buildings. Look at the architecture! I can hardly imagine what they would be worth now or how much it would cost to rebuild them … not to mention the history. Sad to see them go.

Jaan: Can you tell me about the history?

Paula: I can't tell you anything about the history of those particular buildings. I was talking in general about how those types of homes just can't be rebuilt anymore and that there is history behind each and every one of them. The city is tearing down a lot of older buildings, and I'm just sad to see them all go.

Jaan: It is true that every building has a history … possibly of interest to someone. I could find nothing particularly interesting about this building (except that a postal employee once lived there who was convicted of stealing cigarettes from packages intended for troops overseas during WWII).

Paula: Well, I just learned some history! Sad, but interesting. I still like the architecture and the turret on the corner, which would be a pretty cool room.

Marnie: I definitely want the room with the turret on top.

Mimo: A gorgeous house. I wish we could go back to this style of architecture instead of the ugly boxes they put up now.

(Central Mortgage and Housing Corporation 1968-376)

Susan: They could have relocated these houses and refurbished them. That's what they did with a whole block of them where I live now, painted them new colours, put in new wiring and so on. Now they're worth millions.

Kathy: Shame to lose that beautiful architecture.

Steve: So many comments about losing these old buildings, but how many people have actual dollars invested in saving anything? And I wonder how many live in a nice house that used to be farmland in the 1900s? The loss of farmland is the real shame.

Lise: That doesn't refute the fact that it's a shame to lose these buildings! There's lots to regret ...

Guy: I used to deliver the *Citizen* on Chapel Street in the 1950s and saw these particular houses every day.

Janet: I must have walked by them every day going to York Street School in the 1950s. Soon, we won't have anything left of old Ottawa history, only green roofs and coffee shops.

Mary: Hey, Janet, we might have been at school together!

Janet: I went to York Street for public school around 1957-59. Just Grades Seven and Eight. Also Osgoode Public before they built the brand new Viscount Alexander School on Mann Avenue.

Chris: I did the same trio of schools in the mid-1960s. Grades Three through Eight.

Janet: It's amazing *we're* still standing.

A Fish Story!

You see a lot of fishing around Ottawa, and I've always wondered whether people ever catch anything, especially anything big. Well, here's one that didn't get away — a 105-pound sturgeon caught by Paul-Yvon Normand in the Ottawa River at the foot of Woodroffe in the 1920s. I believe you would call this a whopper! Almost three times as long as the kids!

This photo of dad's sturgeon was shared with us by Paul-Yvon's daughter, Lorraine Sarra-Bournet. I'm guessing she might have heard a few fabulous fish stories about this one. Folks in the Lost Ottawa community certainly had fun with it.

Dave: Holy cow, man!

Max: It's a fish ...

Bob: And it's only a baby ...

Tommy: Just a little guy.

Daniel: There's something very fishy about this picture. I think we'll have to "scale" back ...

David: They do grow large! I remember in the late 1970s, a friend's dad and I pulled up and released one from commercial nets that was about 10-12 feet long and almost two feet across the head.

Peter: Was it the 1980s when a man caught a sturgeon in the Deschênes Rapids on the Quebec side, weighing over 200 pounds and measuring over seven feet?

Dan: That fish in the rapids was caught in the late '60s or early '70s and weighed around 110 pounds. He brought it home in a wheelbarrow.

Paula: Wow. Makes me wonder about the myth of the big one still hanging out at Hog's Back Falls ...

Peter: The record for a northern pike up here at Lake Laporte is 32 pounds, 54 inches long, caught by George Myles in 1949. A big S.O.B.!

Randy: Anyone know how old a fish this big would be?

Jaan: Over 200 million years as a species! But that particular fish may also have been very old, maybe as much as 100 years old because lake sturgeon is a species believed to have "negligible senescence." That means negligible deterioration of survival parameters as the fish gets older, so the probability of dying in any given year doesn't increase with age. Mathematicians will say the distribution of lifetimes of these fish is a "Poisson Distribution," with a long tail. Seriously!

Megan: Well, guys, inspiration for your upcoming city fishing expedition?

Chris: New mission this summer!

Judith: Can't wait to go boating ...

Stephanie: I am horrified.

Marie: I'm never going in the water again!

Craig: I understand you can still buy a sturgeon sandwich in Ottawa from this establishment ...

Micheline: Actually it was taken and put in a museum.

Tim: The best part of the story is that there are still 200-pound beasts in the bay, six feet long ...

Owen: Six foot four and 225 pounds actually.

Tim: Oh ya? When did you see that, Owen?

Owen: In my mirror. This morning.

Delivering the Goods

March 24, 2017: 419 likes, 118 shares, 40 comments, 25,876 reached

A whole line of Simpsons-Sears trucks parked in front of the Carlingwood store in October of 1964, when the shopping plaza was less than ten years old. Long before Simpsons (as my Toronto-born mom always insisted on calling it) morphed into Sears, and decades before Sears morphed out of existence.

In their heyday, those guys standing in front of the trucks delivered thousands and thousands of sofas and appliances, as well as presents and parcels all over the city.

Gilles: Ford Econolines!

Mark: Scooby Doo vans! I want one!

Terry: I actually had one of those old Simpsons vans. It was a 1964, so it's probably in the picture!

Mark: That was a busy little fleet, what with the west end of Ottawa growing to include Bayshore, Crystal Beach, Lynwood Village, Kanata and more — and all needing home decor and appliances!

Reid: I remember those trucks ... and when the sign still said Simpsons-Sears.

Rudy: Back in the days of customer service!

(Photo: Duncan Cameron. Library and Archives Canada 3341974)

Patricia: When those trucks would deliver your order and the appliances would actually last 15-20 years.

Deanna: My mom bought a set of lovely, avocado green (!) kitchen appliances at Simpsons-Sears in 1978, when I was four, and we had just moved into our new home. The stove and fridge lasted into the late 1990s.

Nancy: Our home is about 30 years old now, and we've gone through five sets of washers and dryers, three refrigerators, and three stoves already. Where the heck are quality appliances these days?

Michael: Everyone wants shiny stainless exteriors at half the price they paid ten years ago ... not to mention the 47 program modes they can control from their phone.

Deanna: Sigh. I remember when dishwashers were new and they had one with a plexiglass front in Simpsons so you could see how it worked. It was so loud!

Evangelina: I don't think the Simpsons-Sears building has changed much. The mall was extended and renovated, but Sears is much the same.

Joe: Carlingwood was a strip mall at first, with no access from the inside. They built the strip mall into an indoor mall in the 1970s. Years later it underwent the massive renovations you see today.

Norris: I grew up four blocks from there. Before they enclosed the mall, I remember going to the United Cigar Store to buy a popsicle, then breaking it in two on the steel beams outside.

Sam: Even after they enclosed it, you still had to walk outside to get into Sears. There was an awning between Sears and the mall, but they weren't actually attached.

Deanna: That's right, there was a little breezeway from the mall into Sears.

Ken: During the renovations in the early 1970s that turned Carlingwood into an indoor mall, I always had to laugh at the sign that said, "Sorry for the Inconvenience" ... which some joker had signed, "Pierre Trudeau."

Steven: My favourite was the time every "S" went off on the Simpsons sign, so it read "IMP ON EAR."

Craig: Then there was the Loblaws sign that only said "blaw." And the red-lettered Woolworths sign. After an "O" burned out, it never worked the same again.

Eric: Fitting that this post appeared a day after Sears announced it might not survive the year. "Substantial doubt it can continue." Can't say I'm surprised.

Deanna: There is something just so sad about that. A real sign of changing times.

Jeff: Nothing left but Walmart in ten years...

Gordon: Wonder what will go in there next? It's such a big store. Maybe a retirement home for all us old West Enders?

Grandsons of Anarchy

Two boys on tricycles in what looks like Manor Park, circa 1965. Bent on mayhem ... or making the best of it, depending on your point of view!

I remember doing exactly the same thing on my tricycle, trying to make the biggest splash I could. Same again when I got my two-wheeler.

Adam: This looks like what is now that weird five-way stop in Manor Park between Eastbourne, Braemar and Ava. If that's it, those row houses are still there.

Twin: Right, Braemar and Eastborne at the five-way intersection. We used to walk on the fence on the left-hand side.

Patti: Braemar and Eastbourne. Manor Park schoolyard to the right of the photo.

Mike: That's exactly where it is. Our family lived in the house with the green aluminum siding on the northeast corner of Braemar and Eastbourne. If you stood where the kids on the trikes are and turned left 90 degrees, you'd see our house in the late 1970s.

Cynthia: Manor Park, in the era when I lived there as a child.

Chris: This looks like a shot of the corner of Braemar and Glasgow Crescent, closest to Hemlock, where Glasgow did a very quick loop and came back to Braemar. Very close to the place my best friend's sister broke her leg jumping off the school into the giant snow banks of 1970-71.

Gail: I lived in Manor Park three times. Once with mom and dad, once with my mom, and once with my husband when it was the first place we had when we got married.

Mark: Sixty years later the neighbourhood still looks the same.

Jeff: We're all biased, I guess, but there was no better place to grow up in Ottawa (1951-1971) than Manor Park.

Maria: Agreed ... the stables, the pond, the park. No better place to grow up!

Barry: Dairy Queen close by.

Susan: I lived in those red brick row homes in the late 1950s. Good times on trikes!

Cynthia: The days of outdoor play, no matter what the conditions!

Tasha: Loved this season — huge puddles to go racing through on trike or bike!

Marlene: I had a big trike like that. My dad put wooden blocks on the pedals so my little legs could reach the pedals.

Margaret: I remember my big blue tricycle from the early '50s had two little platforms at the back for a second person to stand on.

VR: Do they have those enormous tricycles anymore?

Aliza: I had a trike like that! Oh, how I loved it. Sturdy metal with a ledge in the back to give a friend a ride. It was the 1970s, and my friends had more modern, less sturdy trikes. We all agreed my old used one was the best!

Janet: When we lived on Island Park Drive (mid-1950s), we all went down to the tracks at Scott to watch the train with the dome car go by. My godfather borrowed my trike to sit on and bent the frame. I was crushed.

Virginia: Growing up in Manor Park I so much loved riding my bike through puddles wherever I could find them. But, alas, this can't be me as I had graduated to a two-wheeler long before in the '50s.

Chris: I know I wasn't one of those kids because, being a bit older, I drove a Mustang bike.

Ken: I'm thinking that's a nifty piece of photography with the reflection in the puddle.

Chris: Opening shot for the Grandsons of Anarchy?

The Grace Hospital

Ottawa's Grace Hospital, located on Wellington just east of Parkdale, and shown here in the early 1950s. As a hospital, it was extremely popular with expectant moms and dads, at one point handling more than 3,000 births a year!

The Grace closed in 1999, some seventy-seven years after it opened in 1922, but the site has now been re-purposed as the Grace Manor long-term care facility, and that got people thinking about the circle of life ...

Elaine: I was born there, but in later times I remember there was a sign in the lobby that read: THANK YOU FOR REMOVING YOUR RUBBERS.

Sue: No wonder they had 3,000 births a year!

Elaine: I think they meant rubber boots ...

Jennifer: Well, I guess the other option would've drummed up a lot of business.

(Ottawa Century Book, 1955)

Bev: My two children were born there, in 1959 and 1962, and I still remember that sign after all these years.

Michael: I was born at the Grace. For some reason, it was THE place to be born in Ottawa.

Courtney: I was born there in 1981. I think most of Ottawa was born there!

Laurel: My sister and I were born at the Grace, and so were all my children.

Sue: We had four generations born there. My mom worked there for years. In fact, she graduated nursing school there and I wear her school ring daily.

Gary: I was born there, but they thought I wouldn't make it. I was just over one pound, which was almost a guarantee you wouldn't survive in 1943.

Audrey: Thirteen of my siblings and I were all born in the Grace Hospital and all of us were delivered by the same man — Dr. Erle. My son was born there, too.

Barb: My two youngest were born at the Grace in 1978 and 1983. I lived so close I walked over to deliver.

Lena: My three kids were born at the Grace Hospital. I still remember the sterile green walls and old moulding. My grandmother came to see us and she says, "You are in the new wing." Ha! My dad was born in the "old wing!" Too funny!

Ted: I was born there, my son was born there and my daughter, too. So neat to have different generations born in the same place.

Anita: I was born there in 1959, my husband in 1955, and all of our siblings. As a fund-raiser for the new building, they sold off the bricks for $100. Of course, I just had to buy one.

MaryAnne: My mother, Dr. Anna Sharpe, birthed many babies at the Grace, beginning in 1949 and ending in the early 1980s. She was a paediatrician and obstetrician who practiced in Ottawa for over 50 years and taught at the University of Ottawa. When she died in 1997, we had families coming to the visitation in which four generations had been looked after by my mother.

Joan: But you, MaryAnne, were her "miracle" baby.

MaryAnne: I was indeed. Her only one and very late. She always said she became a better paediatrician after she had her own baby!

Sandy: MaryAnne, I believe it was your mother who delivered me in 1961. All I know is, I was born at the Grace Hospital, and it was a Dr. Sharpe.

MaryAnne: That would have been my mother.

Lorna: My mother was the head dietician there, and I still remember going there as a little girl in the 1970s, especially the old-fashioned elevators with two doors, one criss-cross metal, and the other solid metal.

Lori: Both my boys were born there, one in 1991 and the other in 1994. I will forever remember the wonderful staff, and particularly a nurse named Gillian. She called all babies "little frog" and taught me to handle my newborn with confidence. Listened to the Salvation Army Brass Band practice under my open window. A lovely memory!

Sue: Gillian was a very good friend of my mom's. A wonderful nurse. Now it's going to bother me all day trying to remember her last name.

Sylvia: All four of my children were born there. Dr. Allen first, then Dr. Cromey — and they were actually there for the birth.

Lisa: My oldest was born there in 1998 and delivered by Dr. Legault. It was such a great experience for us! Loved the care we received for myself and my (now 18-year-old) son!

Robert: This is an incredible moment for me, looking at this photo of Grace Hospital. I used to play around there as a kid and the nurses would get the guards to chase me. Later, my wife delivered our babies there, and I remember what good care they took of her.

Teresa: My twins were born there six weeks early and the nurses were fabulous. One twin had to stay three weeks and the other six, so I spent a lot of time at the Grace.

Monica: I was born there in 1954. My birth mother was at the unwed mothers home next door and treated by the doctor who delivered me. My son and daughter were born there as well, and I was in the same room both times.

Caroline: Born there, worked there full-time for one year between children, and then nine years part-time. Best hospital to work in, loved every minute. Three of our five grandchildren were also born there.

Lynn: I worked there as an RN from 1995 until it closed. It wasn't just a hospital, it was a family. I loved working there.

Janice: I worked there from 1982 until it closed. Loved the Grace. All the staff did. Sad day when it closed.

Andrew: But, I guess, those who were born there now have a chance to retire there, too!

Michael: You mean "expire" there, LOL. Coming and going through the same door.

Kelly: If I end up there in my old age, they will have escorted me into the world and ushered me out!

SPRING

Lynwood Plaza

More Ottawa from the Air in this picture, looking down on Lynwood Plaza, with its inverted arches, circa 1959.

The Lynwood IGA, on the left in this picture, became my mother's favourite grocery store after we moved to Nepean in 1966. Brewers Retail was on the right. In between there have been a multitude of stores over the years, but one place a lot of people seem to remember is Leo's Hobby Shop.

Dawn: Heh, heh, heh ... did anyone else try to climb up and slide down the decorative arches in front of the stores?

Randy: Tried to climb them for years.

Cathy: I spent a lot of time sitting in those upside-down arches chatting with friends.

Diane: When I got my driver's license, I went down to IGA to parallel park and hit one of those great white posts!

(Shared by Philip Shaw Bova)

Wendy: My mom did her groceries at the IGA and my dad bought his art supplies at Leo's.

Ralph: Oh man, Leo's. Hobby shop in the front. Barber shop in the back.

Rob: Leo's was a fabulous place for a kid — get your hair cut, and look at model car kits and train sets.

Ian: We would walk all the way to Leo's Hobby Shop from Leslie Park near Baseline and Greenbank.

Allison: We walked from Briargreen all the time. My brother spent hours in the hobby shop looking for model plane supplies.

John: I bought many models at Leo's and even won a contest. The prize was an amazing big Tamiya kit. I was on the top of the world.

Mark: I was really into Dungeons & Dragons and bought my figurines there, as well as Dragon Magazine about role-playing games. On paper … back when we used our imagination! Loved that store.

Kev: Leo's was my fave. Looked at all the models while my little brother got his hair cut. My dad usually got a model we'd work on together. Domenic was my barber … and my school bus driver!

Rick: I remember there was an IGA, the Miss Lynwood Restaurant, a Bank of Montreal, Leo's Hobby Shop, a drug store, a beauty salon, an LCBO and a Beer Store.

Ian: That's where I bought my first "legal" case of beer back in 1973. When asked to provide proof of age, I confidently produced my Ontario driver's license. That satisfied them, and then I was asked what brand and size I wanted. Hesitating, I stepped outside to confer with my still underage friends. The only brand we could think of was Labatt's Blue so I bought a 2-4. We walked the streets of Lynwood drinking the beer on our way to the "pits" across from Bell High. However, we were getting quite loud and someone called the Nepean police, who confiscated the beer and hauled us to the station in Bells Corners where we were each fined $20 for drunk and disorderly. The stiffer penalty was being grounded. Never pulled that stunt again!

Allison: There was an LCBO there too. You looked at lists and wrote the item number on a card and handed it to the man at the counter who'd disappear into the back and return with your liquor.

John: I remember sweating bullets in that LCBO looking at the panels of stock and filling out the little order sheets with a pencil. I guess I must've looked mature (or they didn't care in the early 1970s), because this 16-year-old never got "carded."

Donna: Okay, now I remember this plaza. Where my mom did her groceries at one end — and my dad shopped at the other!

Diamond Bar-B-Q

April 1, 2017: 193 likes, 42 shares, 58 comments, 16,096 reached

Dining out in Lost Ottawa, where the Diamond Bar-B-Q once graced the southwest corner of Bank and Albert. Chicken, ribs, steaks and delicious pies — what's not to like?

I remember having my first steak there when I was about 14. I felt so grown up!

Diane: This restaurant was originally owned by Sol Ages. My mother worked there as a waitress and then manager in the 1950s and early 1960s, and my dad worked three doors down at the Jackson Building. At six years old I would take the streetcar from Westboro (much to the babysitter's horror) and meet my parents downtown for supper at the Diamond, then go to a movie at the Regent or the Capitol Theatre on a Friday night. Good times back then.

Claire: It was the place to go to eat after the show, with the Capitol and Odeon theatres close by.

Marlene: Loved this place after the movies. BBQ chicken-burger with fries and the very, very best rum and raisin pie ever!

Vern: My mouth is watering thinking about all my food memories of the Diamond. In no particular order — banana cream pie, hot chicken sandwiches, BBQ chicken-on-a-bun, chicken livers (where are they now?), and strawberry pie.

Don: Best chicken livers ever!

Diane: Best hot chicken sandwich, too. Their BBQ sauce was amazing.

Frances: It was always a challenge whether to order the chicken livers or the barbecue chicken-on-a-bun. If anyone knows the recipe for the barbecue sauce please let me know.

Sue: My mom's dance studio was a few doors down. After classes we went for chicken-on-a-bun. She must have eaten there four nights a week.

Wendy: A highlight when I was a teenager. Burger and fries topped off with pie.

Fiona: Their banana cream pie was the best I have ever had.

Terry: Great spot. Ate there often with my aunt back in the 1950s. I'd bet money that Boston cream pie came from the National Bakery down the street!

Nick: Actually not. All the pies were made on site by their chef Mike.

Terry: There ya go!

(*Ottawa Tourist Guide*, N.D.)

Frances: I worked there as a cashier from 1969 to 1972. Strawberry pies on Mother's Day got to be a problem, they couldn't make them fast enough!

Deborah: Strawberry pie! We travelled from Britannia to buy it on many occasions.

Gloria: A bunch of us bankers ate at the Diamond every fortnight before the movies. Had my first New York cheesecake ... still the one I like best.

Donna: I loved this restaurant when I worked at 150 Kent (building gone now, like so many in downtown Ottawa). We would go to the Diamond and treat ourselves to lunch on paydays. Their barbecue chicken-on-a-bun has never been equaled. Their banana cream pie was my favourite, too. So many years ago ...

Karen: This was the restaurant I always chose to go to for my birthday dinner with my family. Best hot chicken sandwiches! I was so sad when they closed.

Liz: The one and only time I remember my dad taking us all out to dinner was the Diamond Bar-B-Q for my mom's birthday. That was a BIG deal for us.

Vern: The memory of an event like you have described is one of the joys of living. You made a simple statement, but boy did it shake my soul!

Gail: This is where I met my husband to be in 1962 ... we've been married 54 years this coming July.

Beverly: Classic times, I wish we could wish them back!

Shoppers City West

Looking down on Shoppers City West at Woodroffe and Baseline, complete with its original Freimart store, circa 1961. Freimart would turn into Towers, and Towers would turn into Zellers, if I have all my stores straight.

Plenty of other businesses passed through Shoppers City over the years, but only the Chances R Restaurant survives in the new College Square.

Max: I bought my first blues album in Towers. They had a big record department.

Rick: I saw Chubby Checker play in the parking lot there when "The Twist" was released!

Joe: I saw William Shatner in there in the mid-1970s, either taping a TV commercial for Loblaws or doing an appearance. This is also where I bought most of my albums – starting with the Partridge Family in 1970 and then my first rock album (Boston) in 1976.

Cara: Looks like they were expecting a lot of customers with all the parking they have there.

John: That is a lot of space. So why is everyone parked behind the building?

Nancy: There was a back entrance to the mall.

Beverley: Running across that huge paved parking lot on a hot summer day, in bare feet ... still a vivid memory!

Kathy: The Shoppers City parking lot was so huge it was the perfect place for learning how to drive.

Joe: My dad taught me how to drive there in the 1970s.

Rod: My dad used the parking lot to teach me how to spin in the snow. No curbs.

Karey: I learned how to drive there, too! On Sundays (before there was Sunday shopping), when there wasn't a single vehicle in the lot. Did my share of donuts in the winter, too!

Colleen: Spent lots of time there in the 1960s, when Freimart had pets at the back of the store, including a monkey. You could buy popcorn and then watch the pets with dad while mom shopped.

Judy: A monkey!?

Charles: OMG, I remember the monkey!

Alana: I worked at Towers for 16 years, starting in 1979 – a long time ago. I was still there when it turned into Zellers. Lots of great friendships made there.

Brian: My first job was in the snack bar, making 40 cents an hour in 1966-67. My dad worked Queensway Taxi Stand 4 at the front door.

Bob: I started working full time at the Loblaws there in 1977.

Gary: I worked there in 1969 when it was still an IGA.

Scott: I worked at Top-Valu Gas in 1981-82.

Heidi: Shop-Rite Catalogue Store was my first part-time job, circa 1979.

Charles: There was also a drugstore and a mini-theatre with big screen tube TVs. Didn't last long ...

Roy: My parents would go shopping in Towers and I would go to that little arcade beside the hot dog shop. Wow, memories!

John: I remember getting those hot dogs with the pressed bun, then playing pinball while mom shopped.

Natalie: My friends and I would walk over to get those hot dogs — when we were only five years old!

Diane: In the early 1980s there was also a little restaurant? Burgers, fries, shakes, etc.?

Max: Shoppers Tavern on the northeast corner of the main building?

Maureen: Chances R? Still serves the best coconut cream pie.

Maria: I used to work at the Shoppers City West drugstore and my first boyfriend worked at Towers. After my 10 p.m. shift, I would go to the Chances R for a toasted turkey sandwich, hold the mayo and give me a huge dill pickle. The good ol' days!

Steve: Chances R celebrated their 40th anniversary a couple of years ago.

George: Damn ... is Chances R really that old?

Jeffrey: I used to live at Chances R in the old days.

Alana: Me too. We must be related ...

Remembering the Regent

The Regent Theatre at the northwest corner of Bank and Sparks Streets in 1947. After the Capitol, the Regent was Ottawa's most-palatial and most-loved theatre. Opened in 1915, it closed for good in 1972, when the last movie to play was apparently Walt Disney's *The Lady and the Tramp*.

Wilhelm: I loved that old theatre. I can almost hear the curtains rising.

Heather: My father was the projectionist there and brought me along when he was working the kiddy matinees. If you look closely, there's a tiny window way up near the roof for the projection booth. I have such a vivid memory of looking out that window at Sparks Street, all lit up for Christmas as the snowflakes fell. Magical!

Nancy: I have so many wonderful memories of going to the movies there — then to the Embassy Grill for a treat.

Carla: My parents owned a hearing-aid store at 62 Bank Street, right beside the Embassy, which was across the street from the Regent. Some of my birthday parties were held there. My mum would take four or five of us to a movie, and then back home for the cake!

(Library and Archives Canada PA-110991)

Marian: My dad would take us to the Regent and then around the corner for dinner at the Plaza Restaurant with sundaes for dessert. Then we'd take the bus home from the corner of Bank and Wellington.

Ron: My friend Terry Sheen and I got on the 52 bus in Westboro, went to see *North to Alaska*, then went back home on the 52. We were ten years old! I'd love to see that happen today.

Rosemary: I went there on my first date.

Marilyn: I saw *Wait Until Dark*. Screamed in my boyfriend's ear ...

Nancy: I saw all the Disney movies there like *Mary Poppins* and *The Happiest Millionaire.*

Ian: You lined up outside and, if you were lucky, you got in. If not, you stayed in line for the next showing (two hours later).

Gavin: All the Disney movies went to the Regent, which made no sense given that the Capitol was right down the street and held about twice as many people. My grandmother and I once waited in line for a Disney movie for over three hours!

Angelo: The first movie I saw there was Disney's *Old Yeller*. The last movie I saw there was *M.A.S.H.*

Joanne: I worked at the Regent just before it closed. *M.A.S.H.* was also playing then. I believe *Lady and the Tramp* was the matinee.

Debbie: I particularly remember watching *M.A.S.H.* there with my mom. When we came out, she asked, "Did he say what I thought he said?" I believe that was the first time the F-word was used in movies. Now you can hardly find a movie that doesn't.

Piers My first film was *101 Dalmatians*, which I saw at the Regent around 1960, but I do recall that *M.A.S.H.* played there something like 250 times. A friend was an usher and told me that he'd memorized the entire dialogue because he'd heard it so many times.

Paul: I remember going there as a kid. Smallest lobby and snack bar in the world.

Bruce: Remember the steep stairway in the upper level?

Maureen: I remember the steep stairs in the magnificent balcony.

Paul: The exit stairway going from the second floor balcony to the Sparks Street door was also steep.

Gloria: Do you all remember the wee side door that emptied out onto Bank Street?

Christine: Such a shame these old theatres are gone. They had such class. Today's cinemas have high-def, surround sound, and 3D, but I'd take old-school glamour any day.

A Vanier Tableau

April 16. 2017: 351 likes, 149 shares, and 44 comments, 31,300 reached

While experimenting with zoomable, 180-degree panoramas in the spring of 2017, we stitched together this photo of the corner of Montreal and River Road in 1969. That's when the neighbourhood was still called Eastview, and hence the big "E" on the parking lot sign for what is still called the Eastview Shopping Centre. Eastview would be renamed Vanier a few months later.

Denise: I remember taking the bus with my mom and going here to the Eastview Mall.

Les: I lived in an apartment building next to the Eastview Mall and the Steinberg's grocery store. To the right is the CIBC on Montreal Road where I worked, next to the Scotiabank and across from the motel.

Margaret: I used to live in an apartment building at Montreal and Mona next to the motel, but worked at NDHQ back then. I remember the looong walk from there to work and back during bus strikes!

Peter: My mother shopped regularly at the Loblaws beside the Dairy Queen. On a hot summer day, a child who behaved while the grocery shopping was going on stood a good chance of a reward!

John: I don't remember a Dairy Queen at that location.

Jean: It's right next to the BA gas station in the pic.

Pat: I went to J.O. Swerdfager Public School across from the Eastview

(Central Mortgage and Housing Corporation 1969-68-2 to 68-8)

Shopping Centre and would go to that Dairy Queen on the way home.

Bill: The Dairy Queen was operated by the Delahunt family. We lived on Besserer Street and would walk across the bridge for an ice cream or a milkshake in the evening.

Brian: I remember that DQ very well, but the parking lot was full of wasps, so it was hard to enjoy it!

Peter: There was also an old-style LCBO right across the street (where you wrote what you wanted on a slip and took it to the counter for someone to retrieve the bottle from the storeroom). You got your license plate each year in the office next to the gas station on the far side of Montreal Road.

Brian: The sign on one of the buildings says Ogilvie Flour?

Steve: Yes, Ogilvie. I remember watching the wrecking-ball taking down the Ogilvie Flour building to make room for the Vanier Parkway. There were a lot of slate rocks behind it where we would look for fossils when we were kids.

Michael: Did North River Road always end in that odd cul-de-sac at St. Patrick and Beechwood?

Geoff: River Road used to connect with Beechwood, and was only isolated as a dead-end after the Vanier Parkway was finished.

Norm: Without getting into crude details, did Vanier have the "sketchy" reputation then that it had in later years? How much truth has there been to the reputation, do you think?

Pauline: We moved to Ottawa in 1972 and, yes, Vanier did have a sketchy reputation, but I think a lot of it was hearsay ... or maybe we just didn't hang out there at night in the wrong areas!

Brian: I see Sandy Hill on the far left. That's where my dad grew up.

Geoff: No part of Sandy Hill is visible. The west side of the Rideau River north of Rideau Street is Lower Town.

Brian: I stand corrected!

Geoff: However, real estate agents used to try calling it "Sandy Hill North." Now they stretch things the other way, so the new condos at Waller and Daly are described as "Byward Market." I haven't yet seen Vanier called "Sandy Hill East," but it will come.

Jamie: Rockcliffe South?

Taking the Retro

April 20, 2017: 167 likes, 40 shares, 22 comments, 20,977 reached

So you're standing at the bus stop in Lost Ottawa. You've been waiting for hours and your feet are slowly freezing. Here's what you need – the retro bus schedule app!

It definitely looks old school, but the web app actually reflects the modern schedules. Which is really too bad. It would be so much better if it did historical routes. Or maybe not, because if you ask when that bus is coming the answer is ... never!

Still, those of you who are nostalgic for the OC Transpo of old can get that retro feeling all over again with this locally developed product. You'll still be shivering ... but at least you'll know how much longer your commuter torment will last.

Josée: I love this!

Farrell: Ah, imitating the old NAPLPS videotex systems! By Telidon, I believe.

Jonathan: Does anybody actually know the name of the app? I can't seem to find it so I can't go onto the app store and buy it.

Frank: Right, where do you download this app?

Colin: Correct me if I'm wrong, but this isn't an app, it's a website page.

Luc: But it's still in use at Place d'Orleans.

Josh: Still in use at Place d'Orleans Station, as well as Lincoln Fields, Terry Fox, and Bayshore stations.

Greg: And still a better UI than the official OC Transit App.

Andrzej: Needs to just skip over the bus number you are looking for, just as you get close enough to see it, to be really accurate.

Matt: That's hilarious.

Carol: Bus numbers are changing this weekend ... just a warning out there.

Andrzej: I've been confused about buses in Ottawa my entire life so they could have changed the numbers yesterday and I'd be equally confused.

Christine: So cool. I wonder if it uses GPS times or just posted times (which would be about as useless as those old screens were). I would totally use this app if it linked to the GPS ...

Matt: The old system wasn't based on GPS or any other sort of tracking system. It just displayed the times the bus was "supposed" to be there, which of course was never accurate. So the information was basically meaningless

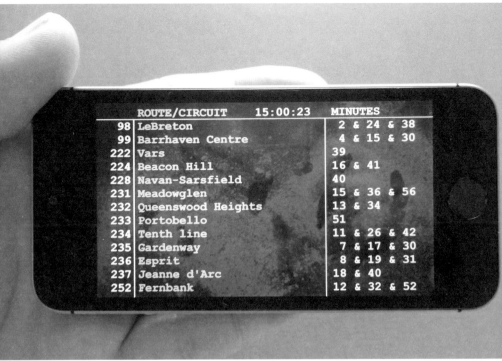

ROUTE/CIRCUIT		15:00:23	MINUTES					
98	LeBreton		2	&	24	&	38	
99	Barrhaven Centre		4	&	15	&	30	
222	Vars		39					
224	Beacon Hill		16	&	41			
228	Navan-Sarsfield		40					
231	Meadowglen		15	&	36	&	56	
232	Queenswood Heights		13	&	34			
233	Portobello		51					
234	Tenth line		11	&	26	&	42	
235	Gardenway		7	&	17	&	30	
236	Esprit		8	&	19	&	31	
237	Jeanne d'Arc		18	&	40			
252	Fernbank		12	&	32	&	52	

and merely provided you with an illusion of the bus being on schedule.

Cassandra: So nothing has changed!

Charlie: Hey man, my grandfather DESIGNED that system. Some respect?

Justin: LOL. How about no. Welcome to the Internet. Where the facts are made up and nothing matters.

Alex: This app just needs a chiller mode to simulate the wait at a Transitway station in the middle of winter.

Sir Robert Boredom

Nepean's school population was still growing at Baby Boomer rates when construction of Sir Robert Borden High School started on Greenbank Road in 1969.

As originally built, the school had some unusual features, including a large sunken foyer covered with carpet, a circular shop wing at the back, hardly any windows in most rooms, and several rooms with no windows at all. The brown brick exterior combined with the lack of windows made the school look like a prison.

"Sir Robert Boredom," we dubbed it as soon as it opened (being smart-alecky teenagers after all) — but it was at this school that my love of history really took off.

Sam: The school actually was designed by an architect who also designed prisons. Almost the same plans were meant for Earl of March Secondary School and Kanata High School.

Nick: Prison architect would make sense. The interior classrooms in the main building were windowless with only two ways out.

Sam: Man, I did not like being in those interior rooms. So closed in, with no

(Photo: Doug Cameron. Library and Archives Canada 3343314)

natural light. There were originally skylights in the upper foyer, but even those were eventually removed because they (supposedly) cost too much for maintenance.

Ian: I attended Sir Robert Boredom, as it was indeed affectionately known, from 1969 to 1973. In those days, it was mandatory for girls to wear skirts or dresses, but since the learning conditions were so deplorable the year it opened, with construction still going on, infamous V.P. "Gizot" relaxed that antiquated rule to allow females to wear pants — to thunderous applause from the female student body.

Debbie: We also called it Sir Robert Boredom. Pretty layout, though, and I think we all enjoyed hanging out in that sunken foyer.

Nick: I remember that area being filled with students at lunch time, music playing through a sound system, and people gathering there throughout the day.

Harry: I went there from 1969 to 1973 and remember the V.P. threatening to put in tile, or even fill the sunken carpeted area with cement, if more respect wasn't shown for the carpet and area in general.

Max: It's tiled now, I'm told.

Allan: The carpet was so much nicer for blasting Genesis, Yes, and disco on Radio SRB.

Kathy: Loved the foyer. My friends would play euchre on their breaks (a game that I found hard to figure out), but the foyer was great for relaxing or even getting homework done (and it was carpeted at that time). The foyer was also where the dances were held in the mid-1970s. Stairway to Heaven was always the last song.

Margot: The carpeted pit was the best place to hang out, but I always thought the round part of the school was strange.

Stu: I loved that circular hallway. Which way do I go to get out?

Kathy: I went to Borden from 1974 to 1979, starting in Grade Nine as a new kid from Toronto. Luckily, I met a great group of people I'm still friends with. I remember some teachers, too. Mr. Klaxon (geography), Mr. Halawani (economics), Mr. Briggs (shops), Mr. Milks (data processing), Mr. Taller (marketing), and Mrs. Bradley (guidance).

EJ: I went there for six years (yes, I went to Grade Fourteen, where I played some more football and hockey and even attended a few classes), then ended up working there for ten years. A lot of great memories. Most of which I can't share online.

Max: This is where I earned my nickname Max and my younger brother was only too happy to see me graduate, because until I left he was always known as Mini-Max. Kids can be so cruel.

The First Dairy Queen

Richmond Road near the intersection with Woodroffe Avenue used to be something of a mecca for early drive-ins and restaurants. It was once home to Ottawa's first Dairy Queen, which was in fact one of the city's first fast food joints.

Here's the sign that stood in the parking lot in 1956, when the Richmond Road Dairy Queen opened, long before there was ever a Royal Burger, Red Barn, Harvey's, or McDonald's.

Caroline: My mom used to take us there if we passed our swimming lessons at the YMCA.

John: If we acted properly in church in the hot weather, then we might get treated to a soft ice cream from DQ on the way home.

Scotty: After church at Our Lady of Fatima, my parents and their ten children would climb in the station wagon or van and head to the DQ.

Sue: My parents would give me five cents after supper to buy a cone. My friends and I would bike down to the Richmond Road DQ all by ourselves at nine or ten years old!

Dale: Me too. Five-cent cone, and another five cents to dip it in chocolate. I also remember riding my bike to Carlingwood to meet my mother. I don't think they worried about us kids the way people do now.

Mike: My dad had a 1951 Willy's Jeep painted orange and blue and he used to pile all the neighbourhood kids in the back from Scott Street and Stirling Avenue, then drive us all up there and treat us to a soft ice cream cone. The Jeep had no roof and no seat belts. Try that today and they'd put him in jail!

Brenda: Constantine's Bakery was just beside the DQ. Then there was Archie's Confectionary, and Shouldice Confectionary on the other side of Woodroffe. A bit further east was a Royal Burger.

Marlene: One of my first real dates. Movie and a Royal Burger! Sigh …

Liz: There were a couple of other fast-food places back near there in the '60s and '70s. For example, on the other side of Woodroffe was Chicken Delight, later Lindenhoff. Beside that was Spindler's Furniture, later Mexicali Rosa's and now the Honda dealership. The Timmie's there was once an A&W where your food was delivered by servers on roller skates. Closer to Parkway Towers was a place called the Purple Cow with such good food in a building painted purple with a huge cow for a sign.

Max: Who was the owner of this DQ?

Neil: Doug Bruin owned it and I worked there for a short time with Bill Moberg.

Billy: I worked for Doug and Flo at that Dairy Queen from 1968 to 1970. They were the sweetest people I've ever known ... I miss those days.

Jule: My brother worked there when Doug, the owner, would give free ice cream cones to the Little League baseball players who won their games. The games were played up behind Woodroffe Public School.

Greg: He would give a milkshake for a home run in the Woodroffe Little League. Regular cones for winning teams.

Penny: I worked for Doug in the summers of 1967 and '68. The job I should never have left — at $1.50 per hour! But I saved enough to buy the engagement ring! I remember the store was only open from the end of April to the first snow.

Molly: Closed for the season. Reason? Freezing!

Max: Should that really be a problem for an ice cream store?

The Highlands of Ottawa

Looking down on the Highlands Apartments, a little north of Montreal Road on St. Laurent in 1973, not long after they were built as one of Ottawa's earliest condo complexes.

From the St. Laurent side, you would never know how swanky they were, with that awesome lake and pool complex out back. Still there!

Jacqueline: I believe Highlands was Carleton Condominium Corporation #16.

Gilbert: My dad managed construction of that project.

Peter: I was a legal survey assistant on the project. Worst part of the job was measuring the inside dimensions of every room in every unit for the final registered plans of the condominium.

Hélène: My dad was the construction superintendent of the project. He was most proud of the man-made lake behind the Highlands.

Jamie: Some units had two floors. Pretty swanky!

Elizabeth: Highlands was the first complex to have high-rise condos, podium suites, two-story condos, and garden condos overlooking the pool. Believe me — I've been living here for 45 years!

Petrus: And if you lived on the podium level, I'm REALLY sorry for running up and down your hallways. I was a child, but I was an '80s child, so ... I Did What I Wanted!

Cathi: I remember going to look at those condos with my parents when I was a kid. They were pretty amazing for the time. Didn't hurt that they were so close to the Red Barn, which is where we went for lunch after.

Judy: I recall being very impressed at how tall these towers were. Very nice!

Petrus: I love that I can see all the windows where I grew up. Whoever posted this, thank you SO much.

Tim: This is our condo development 44 years ago! Our unit is located between the towers facing St. Laurent. Unfortunately, we now face other buildings, but we still have a partial view of Notre Dame cemetery.

Stephane: I lived there for two years and loved it. That was before all the development. It's not the same today, sadly.

Jacynthe: We moved to the Highlands in 1983. It's still beautiful, even if the area has developed intensively.

Samy: The Brittany Apartments to the side look the same, and the pond has always been there, neat!

Eric: One of my first summer jobs was lifeguarding at that pool.

Andrew: I was a lifeguard there for a summer, too ... definitely a few changes in the neighbourhood since that pic was taken!

Tammy: I was babysat in those towers for a few years. LOVED Mme. Gauvreau! But I never got to see that pool.

Peter: However, these weren't the first condominiums in Ottawa — that would be Horizon House on Meadowlands Drive in Nepean, built in 1967.

Sandy: Right. Horizon House is Carleton Condominium Corporation #1.

Mike: I did not know that, I went to Sir Winston School right behind Horizon House back in the '70s.

Peter: I went to Sir Winnie as well. I seem to recall there were some rather sadistic teachers there!

Mike: You're right. We had a certain female gym teacher who was quite nasty. She enjoyed tormenting us. I also had a history teacher there who was very condescending. He reminded us of Major Winchester from *M.A.S.H.*, but not the least bit funny. I'll keep the names out of it.

Sandy: Sadly, Horizon House was built using urea-formaldehyde foam. In 1985, 20 years after it was built, I watched from my front yard as a restoration company removed every brick from the building so the foam could be removed. Owners got a special assessment for $25,000 each, but that year the condos only sold for $15,000 to $20,000! I felt so sorry for the owners!

The Crazy Horse Tavern

Driving out the March Road between Kanata and Carp you'll see a very sad sight. It's the ruins of the Crazy Horse Lounge, once a roadhouse bar of some repute.

This photo was shared by Paul LaHaise who noted the wreck of a sign is still there, although the building is gone. Long gone, really, but the memories remain!

Marc: Where was it on March Road? And when did it burn down?

Lee: Across from the intersection of March Road and Huntmar and it burned down quite a few years ago. There was also a hotel/motel on one side. Had a lot of wings and beer there back in the day.

Christine: Wing night!

Gary: Every Wednesday after hockey!

Mark: How many times did that place burn? At least twice.

Trevor: I recall a few wild Saturday nights there and I was actually there the night it burned down, as a newspaper photographer.

Nadine: It was called the Gypsy Lounge before it became the Crazy Horse. That would have been 1976.

Bob: And before that it was the Hilltop Motel.

Steve: I may have played pool there.

Karen: There was a pool room, after the coffee shop ...

Doug: I could be wrong, but didn't Wayne Rostad play the Crazy Horse?

Dan: His brother Vince did.

Patti: Yes, Wayne played there. Big guy, you couldn't mistake him.

Greg: Saw Delmer and Cecil there, too.

Deb: My uncle used to be the bartender.

Phil: No places like it in the Ottawa Valley anymore. If walls could talk!

Warren: What a hole that hick-trough was.

Maryanne: I've been there. It was a nice place.

Mike: Quite the place in its day.

Wayne: A fun joint!

Paul: A dump! Yeesh!

Cori: I hated that bar. I thought we were somehow cursed whenever we went. I never had a good time.

Dave: Rough and tumble place at times.

Brenda: I recall chairs flying around in the back of the room on one visit!

Cara: It was crazy!

Pat: Spent a week one afternoon there.

Kersty: I met my (still) husband there.

Lawrence: My dad took me line dancing there once or twice a week, when I was 16. I loved it. It seemed like such a welcoming place ...

Tara: I was there once! As a Saint Paddy's Day entertainer. I think I was only 14 or 15.

Jeff: In about 1977, I went to the Crazy Horse when it was still standing. It was just before Christmas, and there were lots of celebrants, and lots of beer-drinking. Party time! Santa Claus was there too. As we left, we saw Santa again in the parking lot being, shall we say, violently ill.

(Shared by Paul LaHaise)

Lib: Candy cane colours?

Jeff: One classy place. Ha, ha!

Grant: A fine distinguished drinking establishment ...

The Mill Restaurant

Ottawa didn't have that many classy restaurants back in the 1970s, but the Mill was one of them. Here's an advert from 1977, when the old Mill (not to be confused with the Mill Brewery that's there now) was still at the zenith of its reputation as a high-end roast beef house.

The food was so good, according to my dad, that they always went there for important business luncheons and dinners when he was with the government. For others, it was a place you went for all manner of special occasions.

In memory of those days, we included a sample menu from the 1970s with the original post, featuring some pretty amazing prices! Alas, the original Mill went seriously downhill towards the end. It closed in 2005.

Max: I'll take the Mill Cut for $9.95 please!

Trevor: Ninety-five cents for strawberry cheesecake!

Pauline: I remember eating there. The roast beef was really good.

John: I miss both the Mill and Friday's on Elgin Street.

Trevor: Both were great options.

Claire: After Al's Steakhouse, the Mill was a favourite.

Nancy: I had a delicious meal at the Mill. It was always a special night to go there! I remember that Ernie Calcutt of CFRA did commercials for them.

Colleen: Went there for a work Christmas party. Loved the food.

Liz: My dad took me there several times in the late '70s and early '80s. Excellent food (in my memory).

Abbie: When I was a child, my family used to go there all the time for birthday dinners and special occasions. Years later I found out my father-in-law did all of the electrical work in the building.

Margaret: I took my parents there for their 35th anniversary. They loved it, sitting next to the big windows looking out at the mill-workings and the river.

Debbie: It's a beautiful spot.

Linda: My first husband proposed to me at the Mill in 1979.

Susan: Lyne and Patrick, remember when your mom and my dad got married? This is where we had the meal.

Lyne: I remember! I also went there with my grandmother Sadie back in the day.

Patrick: Don't remember any of it ...

Dianne: Mother's Day Brunch was a favourite!

Suzanne: My mom pocketed a sugar bowl after dinner there one night. I still have it!

Scott: I remember the Mill as a tourist trap where I took a group of out-of-town colleagues once ... but they liked it.

Sheila: I lost a bet at work in 1976 and had to take two co-workers for lunch. They picked the Mill. I remember it was expensive. I think I was taken advantage of! Ponderosa or the Red Barn anyone?

Max: Unfortunately, the Mill got worse and worse over time and was really bad at the end.

Karen: Probably their last review was from the *Citizen* in 2005 – a scathing description of how awful both the food and the service had become.

Dave: I think the restaurant closed just after that. Deservedly! The new Mill Street Brewery is more casual dining, with good in-house beer and so-so food.

Elizabeth: The Mill was like that nursery rhyme that went "when she was good, she was very, very good, but when she was bad she was horrid." If you went on a good night, the food and service were exceptional. If you went on an off night it was really disappointing.

Marnie: I must have been there on a bad day. You could have used the Yorkshire puddings for baseballs.

Heritage & Roast Beef get together at...

The Mill

Dining Lounge/Salle à manger

Enjoy the finest Roast Prime Ribs of Beef.
Relax and dine in the comfort of the Old Mill,
in our new glass enclosed dining lounges
overlooking the magnificent historic landscaped ruins.

Free Parking   555 The Ottawa River Parkway   237-1311
                 Centre town at the Portage Bridge

(The Key, 1977)

The Rockcliffe Motel

You don't normally think of swanky Rockcliffe in terms of motor hotels. Maybe that's why this picture of the Rockcliffe Hotel from a 1950s tourist brochure was such a hit.

People remembered "the Quarries" out Montreal Road and they also remembered the Rockcliffe Motel, later known as the Crestwood, but what they really loved, however, was the old school telephone number. The one with the old "SH," exchange letters, as used back in the day, when no one thought the human brain could possibly remember seven digits in a row (let alone all the passwords we have these days). The mnemonic seems to have worked, because people sure remembered their ancient phone numbers!

Bruce: I was a kid and lived at CFB Rockcliffe in the early 1960s. I remember there was an area behind the base that people used to call the Quarries.

Robina: The Quarries were up the hill from the base, at Carsons and Codd's Roads, along the Montreal Road.

Francine: I lived on Carsons Road in 1975. There was a quarry just east of us and south of Montreal Road. I seem to remember kids swimming in it. Illegally, of course.

Pat: I remember swimming at the quarry and being chased out by the cops! Great memories!

ROCKCLIFFE MOTEL

OTTAWA'S NEWEST AND FINEST MOTEL ACCOMMODATION

ROOMS WITH TUBS AS WELL AS SHOWERS

RESTAURANT SERVICE — ONE OF OTTAWA'S FINEST

FEATURING FINE CUISINE

BREAKFAST . . . DINNERS . . . SUPPERS

ON OTTAWA MONTREAL HIGHWAY NO. 17

2 MILES FROM PARLIAMENT BUILDINGS

QUARRIES P. O. OTTAWA   TEL. SH 6-0162

(Ottawa Tourist Guide, N.D.)

Ross: I remember the Rockcliffe Motel as the Crestwood Motel, which was located on the southeast corner of Montreal and Carsons roads in the mid-1960s.

Karin: Our family stayed at the Crestwood for a couple of nights in 1970, when we moved from Montreal to Ottawa, and before we moved into the apartments behind the motel. There was a huge old quarry between the motel and a little corner store near what is now Bathgate Drive. I remember the little old lady who worked at the store.

James: I believe the quarry beside the Crestwood was filled in around 1978 or 1979.

Anne: Way back when the Crestwood was still the Rockcliffe, I see it had tubs AND showers! Fancy selling feature!

Max: I like the Rockcliffe's telephone number, starting with the exchange letters.

Jay: The exchange names were REGENT, PARKWAY, SHERWOOD and CENTRAL and I can still recall actually cranking the phone and asking the operator to connect me to my grandmother's five-digit number.

Steve: Exchange names predated dial phones. To make a call you would pick up the receiver, signal the operator and tell her what exchange and line you wanted. When the first dial phones were installed, you could just dial the four or five digits of your local exchange. Later, seven-digit dialing was enforced.

Dorothy: So the motel's phone number was Sherwood 6-0162, meaning 746-0162. Sherwood (74) numbers were in the east end. Central (23) numbers were Centretown. Parkway (72) numbers were west end. Regent (73) numbers were the Alta Vista area.

Aliza: So that's how you used to be able to tell a person's neighbourhood by hearing their phone number!

Beverley: But you didn't say the letters, like "SH."

Antoni: No, it would have been said as "Sherwood 6-0162."

Marc: Ours was Sherwood 6-1678.

Francine: Sherwood 9-4885.

Paulette: Our telephone number was Sherwood 6-1740 for years and years, and then went all fancy and became 746-1740.

Dorothy: I lived on Flora Street between Bank and Kent (and walked to Percy Street School every day). Our phone number was originally 2-3363, then CE 2-3363, then just 232-3363.

Bob: I still remember my childhood phone number, PA 2-6501.

VR: Ours was Regent 3-3432 , later 733-3432.

Mickey: Only someone who's used a rotary dial with the letters on them can really comprehend only dialing seven numbers instead of ten, and getting a fair indication of the neighbourhood you were calling at the same time.

The Ottawa Air Show

Ottawa used to host the National Capital Air Show, which was a great event visited by all manner of strange aircraft, including this F-117 from Desert Storm that delighted visitors in 1992. Looks like a spaceship from another planet!

Terry: The National Capital Air Show debuted at Ottawa Airport in 1990. Before that it was the Carp/West Carleton Air Show. In 2002 the event was completely rained out and that was the last show.

Chad: I remember the last year of the air show, when a B1B swing-wing bomber did a low altitude fly by at Mach 0.9. It was SOOO loud!!

Doug: Kids were bawling, it was so loud.

Mike: I was standing by the fence along the flight line when the announcer informed the crowd that the B-1 had been recalled so it was taking off early. The plane took off and the crowd cheered. A couple of minutes later they played the national anthem and just as the last notes came out of the speakers you could hear a low rumble from the south ... and then before you

(Canada Aviation and Space Museum 28583)

knew it, the B-1 was tearing up Runway 32 like a bat out of hell. You could practically feel the air being sucked out of your lungs. After he passed the crowd, he went into an almost vertical climb. That was impressive for an aircraft that size.

Lloyd: But I think 1992 was the best Ottawa Air Show ever. There was a crazy display by a MIG that even the commentators couldn't follow!

Dan: I remember that! On a low-level pass, the MIG pilot pitched the nose up, seemed to hang momentarily in the air, and then nailed it and disappeared into the blue yonder. The commentator said something like, "whoa ... I don't even know what to call that!"

Clayton: The MIG was awesome. The pilot put his nose in the air, and either shut off his engine or throttled down because he kept moving with his nose up but not gaining altitude.

Richard: Great show, with a Galaxy C-5 on display, bigger than many stores. Two F-4 Phantoms almost broke the sound barrier. U.S. Marines demonstrated their Harrier Jump Jet. My ears still hurt from their vertical takeoff. Man that was brutal.

Jason: I think that was the show where we saw the Harrier as well. Went home smelling like jet fuel.

Yvonne: I remember this F-117 flying over our house. It was really scary-looking.

Michael B: I lived near the airport. Heard something loud. Looked out the window and this thing flew over the house at about 300 feet. Scared the heck out of me! Nearly fell over backwards.

Nick: Saw it blast over Parliament the next day. Circled once, then straight up, at speed. Beautiful day, no clouds. Scary.

Michael: I was there the year an F-117 did a fly-by above some really low clouds ... which got everyone joking about how stealthy it was, alright.

Kij: On the ground they put barricades around it so no one could get a close look.

Kevin: A few of us volunteers got to look at it up close, but weren't allowed to look inside it.

Bill: I actually touched it. Quickly learned NOT to do that again — if I valued my life and freedom!

Sam: I was a kid and asked the U.S. ground crew if I could take a picture. His reply: "If the pilot doesn't kill you, it's OK." I laughed and took the picture. Still have it.

Ray: It is hard to believe that the F-117 came out 36 years ago and was retired in 2008. Time flies, even if this plane doesn't!

Mall Transit

Wouldn't this be convenient? If Ottawa buses actually went right into the St. Laurent shopping centre and took you around to the various stores? I mean, the mall is pretty big, and it's sometimes a long way to walk between shops.

Crazy idea? Could have been a big draw for St. Laurent's Golden Anniversary, which took place in 2017. Hard to believe the mall is already 50 years old!

Fiona: Great idea!

Kevin: Not crazy at all! This is how it's done in Amsterdam, where they have one lane of trams go through their narrow shopping streets!

Tony: It's really only cool to drive through a mall if you're the Blues Brothers.

Rob: Actually, St. Laurent is already the most "subway-mall-friendly" station of them all on the Transitway/Confederation Line. It's attached right to the mall, unlike Bayshore Station with its Indiana Jones-like trek from the platform to the mall — where all that's missing is the giant rolling boulder to outrun!

Martin: The only station that might be worse than Bayshore is Lincoln Fields. Super-confusing after getting off the bus to get where you want to go unless you know the area already. St. Laurent is the best, and I give Rideau second place. Especially now. The closeness of the buses to the dining hall is very convenient!

Carol: That bus is an "Orion." Shorter than the standard 40-footers.

Jeff: They used these buses as commuter shuttle buses back in the '80s. You could call OC Transpo for a pick-up at your door.

Johnny: Oh man, I loved those old buses. Especially the livery on them.

Norm: I always hated them. They'd fill up so quick, we would be late for school.

Christopher: I can't tell you how many times I was late for work, when I was a teen back in the 1980s, because the darn bus was either running late or didn't bother showing up.

Stephen: The picture looks like a promotional display for what was then the upcoming opening of the St. Laurent Transitway station. I would guess it was taken during construction of the station in 1986 or 1987.

John: Before that, there was a more rudimentary station at the north side, near where Toys'R'Expensive was (originally the Dominion supermarket store).

(Photo: St. Laurent)

Stephanie: Back in the days when you could hop on the coloured tiles and avoid the "lava" white tiles at St. Laurent.

Beverley: Is this the only picture ever of a CLEAN bus?

James: Well, the bus in the mall is a 1983, one of 22 new buses bought by OC Transpo that year.

Paula: Had to be 1983 because all buses have the year they were made as their first two digits, unless it's changed?

Griffin: It's definitely changed since then, but was certainly the case in the '80s. I assume they changed it when they realized they had a problem if they bought more than 99 buses built in the same year.

Elisia: Now buses starting with a four are 40-foot buses. The 60-foot Arctics start with a six. When the hybrids arrived, they were numbered in the 5,000s. The double-deckers are in the 8,000s.

Paula: They have double-deckers? Really? Boy, am I behind the times …

Philip: But how did they get this bus in the mall?

Jason: This was a driver making a Timmies run who didn't want to park the bus. Back then drivers cared even less about schedules!

Where Has the Glamour Gone?

What could be better than a movie about a movie palace? That's what this post was originally about, a video featuring a series of photos of the Capitol Theatre in downtown Ottawa.

Located on the southwest corner of Bank and Queen, the Capitol was a movie palace of the old school, designed to give people an experience of luxury on a scale they could never otherwise afford. It's amazing what an impression the theatre made on people over the years, especially the staircase, and apparently the super-elegant washrooms!

Leslie: You know, I would almost have preferred not to have seen this photo montage. Breaks my heart! But the photos Lost Ottawa keeps posting do help remind us to appreciate what we still have!

Erin: Certainly breaks my heart to see so much character gone. Now we just have boxes for everything.

Jennifer: The marble staircase. The chandelier. Those neat settees! So glamorous.

Elizabeth: I used to drift down those stairs as a girl, dreaming of being a princess ... or Scarlett O'Hara. Where did the glamour go?

Carol: I remember this staircase very well. So royal looking ... so impressive ... so hard to describe to someone who has never seen it.

Nicola: The staircase and mirrors made you feel so elegant.

Madeleine: And that's what made going to this cinema so special. The feeling of elegance personified.

Jane: The word "opulent" comes to mind when I think of the Capitol, with its brass railings and marble floors, golden ceilings and plush, red velvet curtains.

Margy: I loved this theatre and remember it fondly, especially the washrooms and the staircase.

Ruth: The washrooms were amazing!

Margaret: I remember my parents taking me to the Capitol to see Burl Ives in the 1950s — when going to the movies was a total experience. Wonderful memories. That staircase! And the washrooms *were* incredible. Pity that it could not be preserved.

Ellen: I have great memories going to the movies with my mom as a young girl. I remember the thrill of watching the big red-velvet curtain open. Watching this video, I can almost sense the excitement I felt then.

Claire: I loved going to the movies there, with that beautiful staircase. My mother would tell us about going to the opera in long dresses, hats, and gloves. I still have her gloves.

Charlotte: It was a beautiful theatre with a lot of class and the last time I went there it was a midnight show. So we put on our good jeans!

Christiane: A landmark where I enjoyed my first opera in the mid-1960s. It was the Canadian Opera Company. *La Traviata* – unforgettable!

George: This is where symphonies performed before the NAC.

Peter: I saw my first concert at the Capitol. It was the Montreal Symphony Orchestra under the young Zubin Mehta in 1963 or 1964. Got me hooked on classical music.

Isabel: Students could get tickets to shows for a dollar in the 1960s, when I saw plays by the Bristol Old Vic and Stratford. *Man of La Mancha.* As a school patrol in the 1950s, we went there for our Christmas party. That stairway ... and the glamorous washrooms!

Roland: I remember going to the Gordon Lightfoot concert, and seeing other stars like Roy Orbison. Such a shame it was pulled down.

(Library and Archives Canada PA-110967)

Ellen: Saw the Hollies in concert there in the mid-1960s. Also the Monkees and Herman's Hermits in concert.

Mike: I remember buying tickets in 1968 to see the Turtles, with Jimi Hendrix as the opening act, only to find out when I got to the door that the concert had been canceled due to uncontrolled circumstances. So much for that!

Gilbert: I saw Jimi Hendrix play live on that stage. I believe that was 1968. Also Cream with Eric Clapton.

Lorny: Also saw Jimi there, second row in the upper seats.

Mike: That was the only concert for which I ever got up at four a.m. in the morning and paid mucho dollars. Jimi Hendrix. Front row center. I remember when some guy rushed the stage to steal his guitar. They ended up in my lap!

Robert: I was at the second show in the upper seats, second row from the back. I always wondered where that guitar ended up!

Lorny: Jimi and Cream played one week apart (or something like that). Couldn't afford both, so I saw Jimi. Glad I did!

Karen: Remember Cream … and Grand Funk Railroad.

Robert: Saw the Hollies and Jose Feliciano in the late '60s.

Jeff: Saw the Who perform the complete Tommy concert there in the late '60s.

Ralph: We were so fortunate to see bands like the Hollies, Jimmy Hendrix, Soft Machine, Butterfield Blues Band, Cream.

Max: But you can't forget all the movies …

Carmen: I saw my very first movie there. *Brigadoon*, with Charleston Heston.

James: My dad took me there to see *Davy Crockett* in the mid-1950s.

Elly: At age 13, this country girl was taken to see *To Kill a Mockingbird*. The chandeliers, the stairs, all so far out of my experience and comfort range. Amazing! So sorry kids now can't experience it.

Piers: I saw so many films there in the 1960s, like *How The West Was Won, Bullitt, The War Wagon, The Rievers, The Dirty Dozen, The Great Race* and some real duds, too, like *Where Were You When the Lights Went Out.*

Lorraine: One of my first dates was at the Capitol, where we watched *Cat on a Hot Tin Roof.*

Allen: I remember seeing James Mason in *Journey to the Center of the Earth* with the safety crossing guards.

Marg: As school patrols, we got free movies at the Capitol every month. Great fun!

Angela: We saw the *Gypsy Moths* there in 1969. It was the last night of the last film shown at the Capitol before it was torn down. A beautiful theatre, I remember the staircase to this day. As Joni Mitchell said: "You don't know what you've got 'til it's gone."

SUMMER

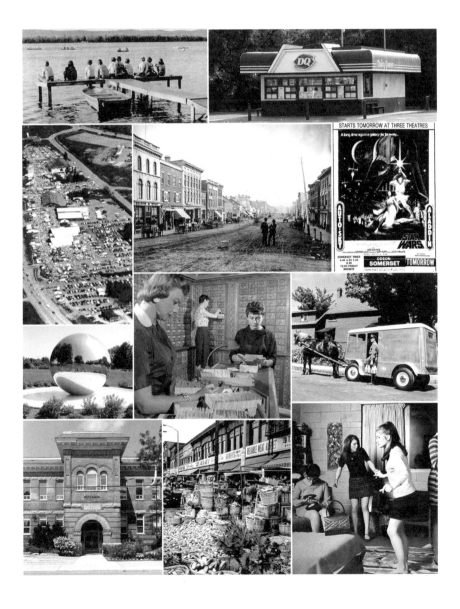

Peter's Pantry

Located just past Lincoln Fields Shopping Centre on the Richmond Road, Peter's Pantry was one of the most popular restaurants in Ottawa's west end. Here's a shot from the late 1960s shared by Michael Moore.

I can't count how many times I went there in the 1970s with my brother and various friends, but I can count how many times I went there by bus. Never!

Bob: Peter's had the best pizza and the waitresses had the shortest skirts. An unbeatable combo ...

Jim: Great pizza and waitresses.

John: Short skirts, decent food.

Shaun: Peter's Pantry had great pizza. I found that the waitresses in their short skirt uniforms did add to the enjoyment of the meal ...

Peter: Not only did the waitresses wear short (but classy) skirts, they would also never write down an order, no matter how large.

Claire: You got it. We had good memories back then ... even myself when I worked at El Toro's.

Judy: I waitressed at El Toro's. No mini-skirts, but the pizzas were better than Peter's.

Karen: El Toro did have the best pizza. Although ... I got sick of pizza while working there, and I always smelled like pizza.

Michael: Some say it was all about the waitresses at Peter's. No! Good food ... Really!

(Shared by Michael Moore)

Diane: I always preferred the pizza from the Colonnade downtown.

Diego: The best pizza in town was always Calabria Pizza on Bell Street. Thank you, Mr. Pasqua!

Heather: The guys loved the waitresses' outfits at Peter's. I loved the Zombies.

Elizabeth: OMG, yes! The Zombies were huge and awesome!

Steve: I had one of their Zombies (the drink) once. Ouch.

Russ: For me it was their Long Island Iced Tea.

Jason: How could I forget the Long Island Ice Tea? It's a wonder I still have a functional liver.

Barbara: They had the best frozen peach daiquiris ... until the machine broke down for good. Now I really am laughing out loud.

Brenda: Loved Peter's ... had many a liquid lunch there during high school.

Lorraine: I actually quit Nepean High School to work there ...

Pat: Ah, yes, Peter's Pantry — where they never checked for ID. Great place for under-age drinking!

Kirk: Wow, now you tell me. So much closer than the Ottawa House!

Tami: They had the best fried zucchini.

Barbara: The best green pepper steak!

Art: Loved their Boston cream pie.

Mark: Seems to me it started as a drive-in/take-out eatery in the mid-to-late '60s, famous for its pizza-burger.

Ellen: My husband and I went there for pizza when it was just a counter and a few stools.

Lorraine: Ellen, I probably made your pizza back then. They actually had two small tables with two chairs each, as well as the counter and stools.

Ellen: We used to order pizza with hot peppers, pepperoni and mushrooms and a dill pickle on the side. Whoever made the pizzas would attempt to put on so many hot peppers that we couldn't eat it. Never happened ...

Karen: As a young kid, my dad would work late, pick up a pizza from Peter's Pantry and drive to our cottage of the time, up past Baskin's Beach. A great Friday night treat!

Anita: Peter's Pantry, El Toro, Chances R, Banana Boat, the Beachcomber at the Talisman, Hunter's Crossing, Frank Vetere's, Mother's, The Corkscrew and many more ... the best classic restaurants and hangouts. All gone now.

Elayne: The Crock and Block in Bells Corners, Town and Country, then Hunter's Crossing, now Big Rig on Iris. The Sly Fox on Carling (former Sampan), Hurley's at Baseline and Merivale. So many restaurants. So many memories.

Daphne: Yes, those were the days, my friend ... but they did end.

The Sphere

At Lost Ottawa we love things that are lost in plain sight. Things that are still right there in the open, that people pass by every day, but which people have still forgotten, or maybe never knew about in the first place.

So, taking advantage of a beautiful summer day, we went to see the National Research Commission's giant mirror-ball along Montreal Road, commonly known as the "Sphere."

Commissioned in 1966 for the 50th birthday of the National Research Council, the Sphere is really quite unusual. It is precisely 4.65 metres in diameter and precisely mounted in a 7.9 metre pool. I really want to know what secrets of the universe those numbers unlock!

Ralph: Try numerology?

Will: The specific molecular density of unobtanium?

Terry: Maybe a pure math person could comment, but I have a feeling that, if you run the decimals on those numbers out a bit, 4.65 divided by 7.9 may be one of those recurring decimal type numbers that go on forever. You know, like one divided by seven. Therefore tied to infinity, the universe and so on?

Elaine: The universe is you.

Max: Ha! I think that was the original name of the sculpture.

Francois: What's particularly special about the Sphere is that it is made of stainless steel so pure, the analogy is that it's like having a box car full of salt with a single grain of sugar in it. At the time it was a major technological feat that earned the NRC great worldwide respect.

Margaret: Decades ago, the government of the day mandated massive budget cuts across the board. The wise and politically savvy RCMP offered up the Musical Ride, knowing it was sacred and wouldn't be touched. The not-so-savvy NRC scientists collected around the Sphere during their lunch break and held a minute of silence. Frightfully poetic, but not so effective. They lost big time, including the research lab of the first Canadian scientist to win a Nobel prize – the John Polanyi lab.

Bram: In the 1970s, I worked as a typesetter at another Lost Ottawa location – Mortimer Graphics. One of the publications I worked on was NRC's "Sphere," which was an in-house periodical.

Michel: My grandfather came into possession of copies of the drawing for the NRC building and the Sphere, the plans for which were made by his brother

(Lost Ottawa)

Arthur Dubois. It's really cool seeing the work and planning that went into such a simple looking monument, including the original idea — which was rejected — for a pool that was square.

Don: I believe the Sphere itself was the work of artist Art Price.

Carri: Art Price used to be my neighbour in Blackburn Hamlet and I remember him telling me about it.

Stephane: In better times, I remember they would turn the Sphere into Santa's face at Christmas time. Now I guess that would offend people?

Charity: I drive past this almost every day. They do put Christmas lights up on the trees around it in the winter and it's really pretty.

Bruce: I remember watching the installation of the Sphere in front of M-58, just after I started working for NRC.

Ratufa: Used to walk by it every day, years ago. It's a surprisingly powerful piece. Always loved it.

Ellen: My dad used to work at NRC. When I was very little, we called it "Daddy's Silver Ball."

Dianne: Drove by the Sphere hundreds of times, and always found myself looking at it. Mesmerizing.

Cecile: I worked at NRC and this was my view everyday!

Beverley: I never knew it existed.

Connie: Me neither.

Thomas: I just want to splash around in the water on a 30-plus day.

Rideau Street, circa 1875

Looking east down Rideau Street, circa 1875, when it seems Ottawa didn't have many telephone wires or electrical poles, but did have wooden sidewalks and some nasty-looking roads. Some things never change?

In any case, I'm pretty sure that none of us would stand in the middle of Rideau Street for a chat these days!

Andrew BA: Is anything in this picture still standing? If the numbers 16 and 18 indicate street address, then that building was on the site of the former Daly building?

Marguerite: I don't think this is the site of the Daly building, but further out Rideau.

Andrew BA: Agreed. There's not enough slope in the old picture to be that far up. If that's the case, then I don't think any of this is still standing.

Jaan: The photo was taken from just east of Sussex.

Andrew BR: Most of these buildings, if not all, are gone. The first one, Kearns & Ryan was numbered 49-51 Rideau Street in 1875. That's where the Chapter's Starbucks now stands. That large number 36 on the building you see further along is at the corner of Mosgrove Street, which if I remember well was the corner of Freiman's Department Store.

Andrew BA: I'm not sure where Mosgrove Street is (or what it may correspond to today), but if Kearns & Ryan and 16 and 18 are now Chapter's Starbucks, then the next building with two floors of six arched windows would be where the western pedestrian overpass used to be?

Jaan: Mosgrove Street was exactly where the remaining overhead pedestrian walkway is today. The building on the northwest corner back then was the old Workman & Co. Hardware Store, once known as "the hardware store at the By-Wash."

Anne: I see even numbers on the place beside Kearns & Ryan.

Jaan: Those were the old numbers, which did not conform to the current standard of odd numbers on the north side. They were changed in 1875, when a lot of the cleanup of Ottawa street names and numbers was done. As Andrew BR notes, Kearns & Ryan was changed from number 14 to number 49-51.

Gavin: The top end of Rideau Street has to be the most photographed street in Ottawa.

Jaan: But to clear up the confusion about the precise locations, here is a list of businesses visible on the left side of this picture of Rideau, as given in the 1873 City Directory: 14 Kearns & Ryan Dry Goods, 16 Fitzsimmons & Browne Grocers, 18 J.W. Ryan Dry Goods, 20 H.H. Brennan Groceries, 36 P. Baskerville & Bros. Groceries, 42 G.R. Russell Furniture Warehouse. Number 36 was on the northeast corner of old Mosgrove Street, which was between Sussex and William. After renumbering, 14 became 49-51, 36 became 89-91, and 42 became 101. At GeoOttawa, you can see the present pedestrian walkway is exactly over the former intersection of Mosgrove.

Lisa: Is this near where the 2015 sinkhole appeared?

Nancy: I think it's forming just beside the dude on the left.

Victoria: WOAH!

Dianne: I love imagining some of my ancestors navigating these streets.

Yvonne: Because this is how our roads still are. Just saying!

David: There's no actual road construction ...

Paul: I think I see OC Transpo starting to dig.

Beverley: There are no potholes.

Yvonne: Thank you for saying that! My suspension is shot, as are the axles. Capital city with "capital" POTHOLES! Happy 150th everyone!

(Library and Archives Canada PA-012540)

Happy Birthday Canada!

The year 2017 marked Canada's 150th birthday, which meant it was also the 50th anniversary of Expo 67. That was in Montreal, of course, but so many people from Ottawa went there (including me) that we decided to post this Expo 67 passport and ask how may people still had theirs.

Turns out that quite a few people still have big memories of "Man and His World."

Leona: I went to Expo 67 as a partying 20-year-old, but the first thing that strikes me on seeing the passport now is the name. I bet it wouldn't be called "Man and his World" if it were held today!

Pierre: My father spoke fondly of Expo 67 several times. Apparently, an incredible moment. Alas, "Man and His World" is a weak translation of "terre des hommes," which has layers of meanings that were, well, lost in translation.

Nancy: I remember having the passport, which you had to get stamped at the different pavilions.

Michael: I still have my white "YOUTH" passport, so full of pavilion stamps I had to insert extra pages midway through the summer. At the time, I was an Air Force brat and my dad was stationed at St. Hubert. A small group of close friends and I would begin almost every day of the summer hitching an Air Force bus to the Longueuil Metro station. First stop was Île Sainte-Hélène!

Gayle: I still have my passport.

David: I still have mine ... somewhere.

Gerry: We can't find our passports, but we do have our pavilion pins. Whenever you went to visit a pavilion, they gave you one.

Glenn: I have a set of Expo 67 postcards and five centennial flags (all different colours), as well as the official Expo 67 guide book, but I don't know what happened to my passport. I do remember getting it stamped at the various pavilions.

Dina: I went with fellow students from Eastview High School and also remember the stamps from the various pavilions.

Sheila: I went with my classmates from Queen Elizabeth Public School on St. Laurent Boulevard.

Doreen: I remember going with my parents as well as my Grade Six class at Queen Mary School. It rained almost all day, but our spirits weren't dampened.

Susan: I went with my family on a cold drizzly day. We didn't care one bit. We had a blast!

Anne: I went with my parents and my sister .... we still have the sombreros we got at the Mexican pavilion!

John: I turned 21 in 1967 and spent most of the summer there! UNFORGETTABLE!

Leslie: We went nearly every weekend and had an unforgettable experience arriving by boat and staying at the marina. World class!

Debbie: I remember going, camping in the makeshift campgrounds, and the excitement of the whole event. I especially remember the Gyrotron!

Jim: I attended Expo 67. It was the first event that I attended with my friend Judy — the start of a beautiful 50-year relationship.

Andrea: My parents both had a passport. They came over by boat from England and managed the British Bulldog Pub. Had the time of their lives!

Beth: I recently visited the Expo 67 exhibition at the Stewart Museum on Île Sainte-Hélène. Good as far as it went. I took a tour of the island and ended up at the former geodesic dome. Memories, memories. So much optimism and possibility ... and fun!

Daniel: I wasn't born yet. But I do have my passport for Expo '86!

(Library and Archives Canada 4943094)

Camp Woolsey

Back in the day, when camps were more popular than they are now, there were a lot of them up and down the Ottawa Valley, in the Gatineau, and out Highway 7 towards Toronto.

One of those camps was Camp Woolsey on the Ottawa River, run by the Girl Guides at the end of the Dunrobin Road, about 40 minutes drive from the city.

This picture of the riverfront was shared by Emma Kent in honour of Camp Woolsey's 80th year of operation. A lot of young ladies have sat on this dock!

Paula: I went to Girl Guide Camp there in 1975. We learned how to canoe off that dock.

Meaghan: I sat on that dock, not as a Girl Guide, but as a resident of the cottages not two minutes away. That's Mohr Island you're looking at across the river. We would take our boats, canoes, wind-surfers, etc., go across, and hang out for the day.

Susan: Went there in the early 1960s. Had a great time.

Lynn: Earned my pioneer badge, among others, in the late 1960s.

Shelley: It was the highlight of my summer when I was ten and the year was

(Shared by Emma Kent)

1970. Years later I did Orca canoe training as a leader.

Trudie: I thoroughly enjoyed going there with my friends Shelley and Francis. I still have my camp hat and my Girl Guide outfit from 1970.

Heather: Late 1970s and early '80s! I remember having to swim with shoes on!

Sarah: My girls love Camp Woolsey. I loved it too, the one weekend I camped there in the '80s. Thanks for sharing this.

Louise: My daughter attended that camp many times and loved it. Now my granddaughters go.

Angela: My first time sleeping out in a tent. With the Brownies.

Chantal: I remember the camp. They had these tents, but the floors were wood.

Natt: I was going to say we slept in tents, but they were more like cabins. Good times! I liked that place.

Kelly: OMG ... spent quite a few summers there, but the winter camping was great fun, too!

Gladys: We did the winter-camping cabins in the late 1990s or maybe the year 2000 when my daughter was a Brownie. Bridlewood Guides. Lots of great snow. My funniest recollection was the constant herding of the girls between the bunk cabins and the main cabin — "Don't forget your hats, mitts, and indoor shoes!" A mother is always in you. Hahaha.

Jen: Remember the spiders, Amelia?

Amelia: The scarrryyy stories I could tell ...

Dan: I went to Camp Echon (a boys camp) and we used to paddle over in the night to secretly meet the girls there!

Becca: In my days, the leaders were on the lookout for "those boys from across the river."

Mike: Worked as a handyman at Camp Woolsey one summer, 1970 or '71. Nice to see it's still open.

Andrea: Not for long. Unless the current Go Fund Me campaign can help raise a substantial amount, it will close, along with all the rest of the camps.

Aliza: They will soon be very lost because the Girl Guides are closing their Ontario camps. Not enough people are sending their daughters, so the Girl Guides can't afford to keep them going. I feel sorry for the children. They're missing out.

Bob: I had heard that the Girl Guides can no longer afford to run the camp.

Melanie: Woolsey is one of the only Ontario camps that is constantly booked, but it's costing a lot for the maintenance and repairs needed to keep it running.

Paula: Noooooo ... please don't close a camp that has so many great memories!

Miles for Millions

July 16, 2017: 177 likes, 37 shares, 43 comments, 19,645 reached

Although you might not be able to tell in black and white, those who were online could see this was a photo of a bright orange Plymouth Duster at the corner of Maitland and Tara Drive in the west end, with Trinity United in the background, circa 1970-71.

Shared by Wilhelm Gere, the photo was taken during a Miles for Millions charity walk. Someone clearly wasn't keen on walking!

Brian: Is the roof still like that on Trinity?

Sarah: Yes, and I always think of a hydro-electric facility whenever I see it.

Anna: Me too! Haha.

John: Is the car a Plymouth Duster, or a Dodge Demon?

Wilhelm: I think that's the Duster logo on the back. I had a brown Duster. Thing never would start in the rain ...

Mark. Taillights on the Demon were vertical not horizontal, so definitely a Duster!

Jason: I'd like to see modern cars pumpkin orange.

Wilhelm: They came in all kinds of yucky colours. The one in the picture was called Tor-Red.

John: True story ... starting with a groom who owned a 1971 lime-green Duster. He, an usher, and me (the best man), left from Peterborough at 5:30 p.m. on a Saturday afternoon, and arrived at his fiancée's in Vancouver at 9:15 p.m. on Monday evening after 55.75 hours of driving non-stop. We were stiff and sore, but relatively unscathed. We were then 22. We are now 67. If we tried it again, we would be crippled for the rest of our lives!

Max: I could have used a Duster on my Miles for Millions walk ...

Janet: I did Miles For Millions twice. I remember being told afterwards that my grandparents thought I should be pulled out of the walk because it could be dangerous for a 14-year-old to be out late! Thank goodness my parents didn't listen to them.

Patricia: I walked Miles for Millions many times in the late 1970s and early '80s. Then they changed the name to Metres for Millions and it died. So much for progress!

Tasha: "Metres for Millions," just didn't have the same ring.

Margaret: I managed 20 miles before the blisters got too bad, but I remember raising something like $35 and I was proud of that.

Louise: Walking 40 miles in a day ... for pennies. But with a lot of folks sponsoring you at five or ten cents a mile, those pennies added up. We felt like we were doing something good.

Wanda: I did this walk a few times ... with no prep, cheap canvas sneakers, no water ...

Wilhelm: The first year I went it was stinking hot and that was the year "Walking Across the Desert on the Horse With No Name" came out. I must have heard it dozens of times that day from people with portable radios set to CFRA. I'm still sick of that song!

Jan: I did the Miles for Millions walk three times. Wrecked my feet.

Gerald: I was in this one. Sore knees, more than feet.

David: All my toenails fell out.

Tom: I remember I was so stressed getting pledges. I wish I didn't remember the day after — blistered and sore!

Susan: I went with my friend in the late '60s. That night we went to Pineland and danced, then spent Sunday in the backyard with our feet in buckets of ice-water.

Andrew: I remember completing the 40-mile walk at sundown at Sussex and Rideau. With wicked blisters.

Dave: Still have the blisters.

Cynthia: I walked the whole thing and ended up at the train station. I was 13 at the time and had to bum a dime to call my brother to pick us up. He said, "Can you walk down the street to meet me?" Blisters upon blisters!

The Opening of *Star Wars*

It was Thursday, July 21, 1977, when this ad appeared in the *Citizen*, announcing the premiere of the first *Star Wars* movie – the start of the cultural revolution that's still going on!

Amazing to think that such a "block-buster" only premiered at the Somerset Theatre and two drive-ins.

Garry: Man, oh man. I remember lining up many times to watch this at the Somerset, just off Bank Street. Good times!

Mark: I was there in line on opening night with my friend Eramelinda.

Bob: My friend Jane and I were there in line on opening night. I was the fan ... she was humouring me!

Steve: Two friends and I saw *Star Wars* at the Somerset the first day it was in town. I think it was a Friday night show that started at 7, so we got there at 3:30 – we were the first three people in line. I had no idea what the movie was about before we went in.

Keith: I remember the line-ups at the Somerset that year. Went three times. First show, I got the far right seat in the front row!

Michael: I remember sitting with friends on the little hill just west of the doors, waiting for the 2:00 p.m. showing the first Saturday. I went back five or six times on my own ... the nerd was strong in me.

Wendi: I saw it at the Somerset. One of the best days of my life!

Angus: I saw it five or six times at the Somerset. In fact, I saw most of the good films of the day there.

Anthony: Saw it over twelve times at the Somerset!

Patricia: Saw it over and over and over with my friends. Watched three or four showings a day for weeks!

Patrick: I remember the opening scene vividly, mind blown and hooked on film ever since.

Dave: I saw it at the Somerset when I was four. Still remember the garbage compactor scene most vividly!

Sean: Saw *Empire Strikes Back* opening day. Remember lining up in the alley between the theatre and the bank next door.

Laura: I remember waiting two days for *Empire* when I was 12. We ended up being second in line!

Michaella: I remember standing in line for eight hours to see *Return of the Jedi*.

Pino: And I was with you. The line wrapped all the way around the corner and onto Maclaren Street.

Sheldon: I was in line for *Return of the Jedi* on premiere night, with spotlights and everything outside the Somerset, when this limo pulls up and Prime Minister Pierre Trudeau got out with his sons for a movie night.

Steven: I was at the same showing ... and was back at 8 a.m. the next morning to see it again!

STARTS TOMORROW AT THREE THEATRES

A long time ago in a galaxy far, far away...

(Ottawa Citizen)

Alex: I remember cutting one of these ads out of the paper that summer and saw *Star Wars* at the drive-in.

Shane: I saw it at the Aladdin.

Brent: Saw it at the Auto-Sky. One of my most vivid childhood memories.

Graham: I remember my father taking me to the Auto-Sky to see *Star Wars* in his brand new Plymouth Volare.

John: Oh, how many times we snuck in the back of the Auto-Sky that summer!

Sheila: I remember seeing it at the Somerset, like everyone else having no idea what a pop culture phenom it would become.

Tasha: I've seen these "memes" about people who've never seen *Game of Thrones*. They should have one for those who've never seen a *Star Wars* movie. Back then, I thought it was a movie that would come and hopefully go ... far, far away.

The Byward Market

Ottawa's Byward Market in 1977, when things looked a little different than they do today, particularly this area where vendors used to pile their fruit and vegetables up to the sky.

Silvye: This is exactly how I remember it ... in 1977... ouch!

Joanne: I remember this from shopping with my mom in the 1970s. She used to go shopping on her lunch hour and lug two-dozen cobs of corn home to the west end on the bus.

Joe: This is my childhood. I remember driving down with my dad to buy fresh fruit and vegetables to stock the windows at our family's grocery store.

Isa: I used to go to the market with my parents every Saturday. They would buy vegetables and chickens. Then we would go to Freiman's for a malt.

Laura: Went there every Saturday morning with my dad. It was a one-stop-shop for fresh local fruits and vegetables, local butcheries, the huge Lapointe fish market, and the bakeries. Such a busy place — and those amazing malts from Freiman's!

Marion: I remember when quartered pigs were on display. Farmers sold their chickens and eggs and produce in bushels, delicatessens were in abundance, ladies sold flowers, streetcars clickety-clacked their way up Rideau Street. There was so much activity and atmosphere.

Marion: We went to the market with our parents every Saturday morning. They would buy vegetables. Next we would go to the deli and buy a variety of cold cuts and breads. Then we would go home and have a feast, tasting all these different delicious foods.

Joe: You could buy livestock as well.

Karen: I remember them selling live animals on York Street. Chickens, rabbits, etc.

Gillian: We bought our two pet rabbits from there.

Elizabeth: We bought a pair of ducks. Gronk and Daffy. Can't do that now!

Kathleen: As the saying goes, "the good old days."

Max: Unless you're vegan!

Joanne: In the 1960s my godparents had a stall right outside Lapointe's Fish Market. We would go there every Saturday morning. My cousins and I would watch the stand at lunch so our parents could go for a beer at the Lafayette Hotel ...

(*The Key*, 1977)

Michael: It was such a seedy, sketchy, wonderful experience back then, not this sterile tourist clap-trap of today.

Mark: Vibrant and busy. As opposed to the over-regulated city-approved wasteland it is now.

Al: I think one big problem is that the food vendors got kicked out of the Byward Market building and replaced by craft stores, boutiques and eateries. Decades ago the building was occupied by butcheries and other local food vendors. This is what people want to go back to. The city should reduce the rental fees to make it possible to have a profitable business in the market building itself.

Geoff: The problem with that solution is that produce is a seasonal business and the building is there year round — no easy answer.

Daniel: And there are, in fact, plenty of butchers and bakers in the market, and the businesses in the market building have been quite successful.

Tania: I was born in 1977. I've gone to the Byward Market ever since I was a kid, and still go when I can. It doesn't look like the picture anymore — which brings back good memories — but there's a cheese shop and a deli, talented buskers and bakeries. It may not be the same as it was back then, but I still have a good time now. There is a lot to enjoy!

Leslie: Not sure why there is so much sadness in so many posts. The vendors sell local food. It's still fun. The market is vibrant. There are even Beavertails now. It's all good!

Groovin' the Carleton Res

July 27, 2017: 482 likes, 56 shares, 52 comments, 29,221 reached

Life in residence at Carleton University circa 1969, where you could have your own dance party and the biggest question facing you was – what 45 record to put on next?

Paul: The Monkees?

Rudy: The next 45 I would have put on the turntable would've been the Guess Who – "These Eyes." Or, how about Sly and the Family Stone – "Hot Fun in the Summertime!"

Margaret: Wow! I remember those days in the late '60s and early '70s. Listening to The Youngbloods and Elton John or Muddy Waters!

(Carleton Raven, 1969)

Wilhelm: You could turn on the TV and watch "Saturday Date" on CJOH.

Robert: "I'm so young and you're so old. This, my darling, I've been told. Oh won't you stay with me Diana?" Ottawa's own Paul Anka.

Wanda: They are playing 45s on the record player. One song per side of a vinyl record. That's what the girl on the left is holding … or maybe some of you young folk you know this already? How about you, Jenny?

Jenny: Yeah! My grandpa had a thing called a "record player" and he would play these things called "records" sometimes!

Carol: I was at Carleton in the '70s and the rooms looked exactly like that.

Jenny: The residence rooms still look exactly like that.

Rob: Which residence is it?

Dominic: Looks like Russell, or Grenville.

Hunter: Could be Russell, Lanark, or Glengarry. They were all identical inside.

Carol: I thought it might be Lanark House.

Niki: I lived on 4th Renfrew ("4th Ren," we called it) in 1988-89 and 1989-90. My room was exactly like this.

Wanda: The curtains are different, but those bookshelves on the wall tracks were there when I was. And who could forget the lovely cinder-block walls?

Laura: Bookshelves were still there in 1999.

Caroline: It reminds me of my friend Kay's single room … only the bed isn't up on milk crates!

Ann: Pretty sure that room is in Lanark Res — where I was in 1969. I remember decorating the cinder block by gluing coloured popcorn to the grouting.

Amanda: This could definitely be my res room! We used to throw random dance parties. Attendance was quality over quantity!

Cindy: I was going to say I was the one studying, but then I see she's checking out the 45s!

Sharleen: A couple of these girls look familiar from my res-1969 days!

Christian: Rockin' the mini-skirts, eh?

Fran: Familiar hair, familiar clothes!

Dianne: The clothes, the hair … the knees!

Cindy: Shocking!

Cheryl: Flat shoes look so much cuter with mini-skirts, unlike spikes which just look sleazy.

Dennis: Far out man!

Anne: Groovy!

Tunney's Pasture

July 31, 2017: 360 likes, 126 shares, 48 comments, 33,316 reached

Up in the morning and off to work — at the Tunney's Pasture Complex, built as part of the Gréber Plan of the 1950s for distributing government offices to multiple remote campuses around Ottawa and Hull. Thousands and thousands of people have worked there over the years. Many of them in that tall structure going up, which appears to be the Brooke Claxton building, circa 1964.

Dave: But you know, probably even more Ottawans learned to drive in Tunney's Pasture than ever worked there. Any given weekend, it's completely deserted except for those nervous 16-year-olds creeping along ...

Chris: I always thought "Tunney's Pasture Complex" sounded like some oddly specific mental condition where people are afraid of standing in large, open fields.

(City of Ottawa Archives CA008697)

Don: Was there actually a farm there owned by a family named Tunney?

Anita: I lived at 203 Parkdale from 1940 to 1963. The Tunneys lived at 201 Parkdale, and I clearly remember Mr. and Mrs. Tunney sitting on their front porch, watching us play on the street. I don't ever remember the pasture being used for anything ... except as a wonderful playground for us kids.

Carmen: I was born at 62 Caruthers in Mechanicsville, very close to Tunney's, and lived there from 1943 to 1955. I remember there were many very poor people living in Tunney's Pasture. A lot of them were my friends.

Anita: I remember there were small homes along the river, all grouped together. Most were makeshift with dirt floors, later all demolished in preparation for the Parkway.

Carmen: I remember going into a one-room shack with a mother and daughter living there. They had a single bed and a kitchen table with two chairs and that was it. I knew another family who also lived in those shacks, most of which did have dirt floors. That was in the late 1940s and early 1950s. I will never forget it.

Larry: I lived on Hinchey Street, last block before the river. We rented from NCC and had to move for the Parkway, although the house stood empty for quite some time before construction got started. Interesting neighbourhood at that time, for sure!

Dianne: My experience working at Tunney's was a little like *Joe Versus The Volcano*. No windows! In winter, it meant entering and leaving work in darkness, but I also made some good friends there.

Bram: I remember trying to do bacteriological testing in a lab without air conditioning.

Ian: I think there also used to be a nuclear reactor on the site? No wonder I couldn't drink the water when I was at Claxton!

Jo: Hank, did we really work there for decades?

Hank: It only seemed like work!

June: I spent 37 years there, but it does seem like a very long time ago now.

Hank: Was Walter Duffett Chief Statistician when you started?

June: Yes, followed by Sylvia Ostry, but what I remember most was being interviewed by Assistant Director Nesbitt, smoking his pipe as he asked me to spell St. Catharines. This was the tricky question ... Well, I nailed it and the rest is history!

Catherine: I worked at Tunney's Pasture for Statscan in the summer of '85. My most memorable moment happened the day my "supervisor" was arrested on the floor for dealing drugs!

Rob: Drugs-can?

Catherine: Yep ... and they weren't doobies!

The Card Catalog

Here's one for all you librarians in Ottawa, featuring three ladies working in the Library of Parliament in 1957, back in the days when there were no desktop computers, no Google, and searching the catalog meant searching the "card catalog," which also had to be meticulously maintained.

Imagine the librarian's joy! Putting one card for a new book in the middle of title drawer BAF-BAG, another in the appropriate author drawer, and another in the subject catalog. Weeding the catalog … all done by hand. What fun! And the Library of Parliament is thought to have had over a million items at the time!

Chantal: I actually filed cards in this catalogue.

Paulette: I had to check filing for two hours a week in the French catalogue.

Sylvie: My first job in the Library was typing and filing cards for this very catalog. I spent quite a few hours in there.

Teresa: Imagine TYPING all those cards! I'm so happy to be a cataloger now we use MARC coding on computers.

Janet: Back then there was also the Dewey Decimal System. So exciting!

Susanne: An hour at the catalogue drawers filing meant you moved away from your desk and maybe had a chat. But I hated typing those cards because of the rigid rules about spacing … and the always looming threat of making a mistake in the last word.

Carole: I loved looking for a book in the card catalog, opening the drawer and fingering through all the books that were available. Computer searches just aren't the same.

Helen: I agree. There isn't the same sense of satisfaction looking things up on the computer. It was the "thrill of the hunt," knowing which card catalogue to use, or where to look — especially using the Dewey Decimal System!

Gloria: Reminds me of my days working at the National Library of Canada, Reference Division in 1960. I did a lot of filing in those little drawers!

Lori: I remember the shelf list at the National Library in the 1970s, with stacks of cards on top that just wouldn't fit in the drawers.

Mary: When I worked for Labour Canada, we also had the cards. Computers weren't in yet.

Patricia: I spent a lot of time at NRC on Sussex Drive filing those cards and looking up books.

MaryAnne: I loved the CISTI library, searching among the stacks with the glass floors!

Carol: I used to avoid the catalogue and just memorize where the books were when I worked reference at the Ottawa Public Library.

Melanie: Not so long ago, when I was in Grade Seven, I sorted books and cards after school. I had volunteered at the Rosemount Branch library, a couple of doors down from Connaught Public School. I hated that job! So boring. The best part was the back rows of books, where I would imagine scary stories to keep my brain occupied.

Sylvie: I think that the beautiful lady on the left is Madame Quirouette, maiden name Caron. She was there in 1973 when I started. She was the sister of Estelle Caron (chanteuse pour Les Troubadours).

Ted: Killer hairdo on Madame Quirouette. Pearls, clip-on earrings, and a bracelet for work. Where do you see that today?

MJ: With a quick look, you would think she was a young Doris Day!

Marnie: Back when we used to dress up to leave the house, whether going to work, shopping, or just walking. We did not step into the street looking like slobs.

Jenny: Unfortunately, we don't see everyday dress-up anymore. Just jeans, short shorts, and braless wonders.

Max: Hey! I just paid $300 dollars for my sneakers!

Old School DQ

One of Ottawa's oldest Dairy Queens is this one, located on the southeast corner of Merivale and Clyde.

It opened in 1959, it's had a makeover, it has the modern DQ logo on the front – but don't let that fool you. This one is Old School, Baby! No drive-thru. No place to sit down (except for those tiny benches on the side). No burgers, no fries. Just ice cream and drinks. Walk up to the window and order some memories!

Patricia: The first sign of spring in the Ottawa area? CJOH reporting the DQ at Merivale and Clyde was about to open.

Valerie: A six p.m. news event on CJOH.

Roisin: The opening of this DQ defined the start of a summer, and its closing always marked the end.

(Lost Ottawa)

Wilhelm: As kids, we waited for them to take off the boards and reopen.

Rick: And there was always a line-up when it opened up for the year.

Tom: We used to ride our bikes up through Parkwood Hills — and there used to be a farm on the way — to get to DQ for a ten-cent cone. That's when Merivale Road was basically a dirt road.

Karen: We went to this DQ every Sunday after church, when a small cone was five cents.

Mary: We would walk there from Carleton Heights for a chocolate dip cone.

Niel: Trying to find some shade on those hot July days ... to eat that soft dipped cone before it melted.

Wendy: I remember going in pj's on Sunday nights back in 1965. We got the kids' cone. Dad had the milkshake.

Gayle: I so remember my mom and dad taking me, my brother and my sister. Somehow we always got the ice cream ... and they got the banana splits!

Kathleen: In the 1980s, whenever my parents said we were going for a drive, I knew it would end at the Merivale DQ. Mom usually got a rum-raisin milkshake and dad got the mint-chocolate chip.

Lisa: This DQ at Merivale and Clyde is the one I grew up with in the 1980s and '90s. As far as I can remember, it never had burgers and fries, just ice cream. It actually shocked me to find out that DQ had burgers and fries when I was older.

Bruce: I remember the first time I went to the DQ on Bank Street near Grove. I was shocked at the idea of a DQ open in the middle of winter where you could get a hamburger, too.

George: Only ice cream products in the beginning. Burgers and fries didn't show up until much later.

Andréas: I love that classic feel, man. Forget those burgers and fries, I want ICE CREAM!

Harry: This is the DQ where I fell in love with malted milks. Can no longer find them anywhere.

Linda: My faves have been gone for years. Mister Malty was heavenly.

Pegi: In the 1970s, my fave was Double Delight, meaning two scoops with strawberry sauce on one side and chocolate on the other, covered with nuts and whipped cream. They took it off the menu!

Faye: I used to have a butterscotch sundae.

Claudia: I stopped going to DQ when they discontinued the butterscotch dip. Ain't nothing like that butterscotch!

Sarah: I didn't realize they dropped it. That's a shame.

Valerie: It seems like just yesterday ... oh wait, that was yesterday!

Mutchmor Public

Here's the Romanesque-style facade of Mutchmor Public School, located at the corner of Fifth Avenue and Lyon Street in the Glebe. Designed in 1895 by prominent Ottawa architect E.L. Horwood, it's had some additions and alterations, but it's still a very handsome building today.

Sandy: I taught in one of the original classrooms. It had a staircase to the attic. The tin ceilings were beautiful.

Tasha: I remember the tin ceilings in Room 2 (and why do I remember the room number after all these years?). Miss Morphy's Grade One class had them, as well as the old desks with bench seats bolted to the floor.

Linda: I went there from Grade Two through Grade Six, and later had a spell as a supply teacher and kindergarten assistant before going back to university. It was an odd feeling teaching in the school where I had been a student. Even stranger because my youngest brother was a pupil!

Rob: I still have my first report card from Mutchmor, dated 1953. I love the comment from the teacher on it saying, " ... enjoys a good fight."

Dan: I went to Corpus Christi in the late 1950s when we had some great snowball fights with Mutchmor across Fourth Avenue. Of course, the Irish Catholic kids always won.

Bill: Some tough dudes attended Mutchmor in the 1970s. The Glebe wasn't so posh then.

Rick: I remember an older kid pushed me into the flag pole. Had to go for stitches. Times have certainly changed.

Tasha: I remember the house next to the girls' yard on Fifth Avenue had a lovely wall that was good for bouncing balls off of — we used to have a lot of games that required that. It also had an older lady who was always complaining ...

Pam: No one bounces balls off walls anymore!

Barbara: I remember someone daring me to stick my tongue out onto the steel post on the fence — teacher had to bring a cup of warm water to get my fool tongue off. Dumb? Or ... anything for a dare!

Robbie: Mutchmor is the first place I learned to "drop and roll" if caught in a fire, but most of all I remember the strange day that Kennedy was shot and they sent us all home. It was eerie. First time I had ever seen the neighbours all out on their porches talking to each other, all the way home.

Karina: I went to Mutchmor for flute lessons after school. My flute teacher was shaped like a flute, but with a moustache. He wore his shirt undone to the third button, exposing chest hair. I still feel queasy thinking about it.

Chris: I recollect being chosen to run the mimeograph machine in the front office.

Sarah: I got to use the big machine in the office, too (in the 1980s). I can still remember the smell of the blue paper.

Brian: The Xerox copier also smelled great.

Sandra: The store across the street was Dworkin's. Great penny candy!

Paul: Thanks for reminding me of Dworkin's! We stopped in almost daily for a few pennies worth of candy. Black balls!

Gloria: Later Yaghi's. All lost now.

Cathy: I grew up on Fifth Avenue and went to Mutchmor from 1965 to 1971, when Miss Butler was principal. I was a member of the school patrol, a very important job!

Tasha: I was there during the reign of Miss Butler. I can still hear the sounds of her heels as she walked the deserted halls during class.

Wendy: I had Miss Butler and Mrs. Perry for Grade Six in 1962.

Susan: I had a few run-ins with Miss Butler and I can still hear her say — "wipe that look off your face!"

The Clark Dairy Man

Deliveries by horse and wagon were one of those basic rhythms of city life back in the day, and here's a photo of a heroic-looking Clark Dairy Man delivering the milk from a horse-drawn wagon somewhere in Ottawa in the early 1950s.

This post got a ton of comments from people who remembered the milkman, the bread man, the ice man, cream in the bottles, "helping" the drivers with deliveries, and more.

Peggy: Can you imagine this rhythm of life compared to today's frantic pace on streets and highways? You feel relaxed and sane just looking at the picture. Working with some beautiful animal, happy and well kept ... what could be more soul-enriching than that! I want this job!

Cheryl: I lived on Bell Street for a couple of years. Every morning I would listen for the "clip-clop" of the horses and the clink of the glass bottles. Such a pleasant memory. I was only five years old.

(Canada Science and Technology Museum 76-4832)

Barbara: We had our milkman, bread man, veggie man, ice man, coal man, all delivering by horse cart. Good old days!

Janice: I loved horse-drawn milk delivery and remember giving the horses carrots when they came by our house on Third Avenue. We called our Clark driver Mr. Clark! Don't know what his real name was ...

Deborah: My uncle Les Clark worked for Clark Dairy. He delivered milk to our house by horse in 1957.

Bonnie: Walter was the name of our milkman in Old Ottawa South in the 1940s and '50s.

George: All the kids on my street would race outside with sugar cubes to feed Walter's horse. I sometimes wonder if we didn't give the horse diabetes!

Anne: We lived in the Glebe. Borden's was our dairy and the horse's name was Towser. Fed Towser many lumps of sugar!

John: Our milkman was Cliff and his horse was Silver. I was his "helper" on Saturdays in Hintonburg in the late 1940s.

Trish: I remember Silver. And also how the milkman would give us hunks of ice from his wagon on hot summer days.

Dan: I remember the milkman at my grandmother's house on Glenora Street. He would let us kids ride in the wagon up to the corner, then give us a piece of ice and send us home. Kinder gentler times!

Barbara: I used to ride with Johnny the Bread Man so I could hang out with his horse, Rosy.

Bob R: On Drummond Street in Ottawa East, the horse's name was Bob. I would meet him at the end of the street. The bread man would lift me up onto a little saddle and I would ride the horse as it stopped and started at each house on the route. The bread man only had to enter and exit the van at the correct house because Bob knew the route. At the end of the street Bob would stop and wait until I was lifted off.

Carole: We lived in Centretown at Arlington Avenue and Kent. Our Walker's bread man would let my brother and I hold the horse's reins. Not that we needed to because, as Bob just said, the horse could do the route all by himself.

Marnie: The horse knew the route better than the driver.

Jeff: The horse probably knew what each customer ordered!

Jacques: My grandfather and great-grandfather both used to deliver the milk in the Aylmer-Lucerne area. Apparently, by the time they finished their routes, they were so drunk the horses took them home by themselves ...

Bob S: My dad delivered milk for Central Creamery in Renfrew. All the customers would give him a drink the day before Christmas. Good thing the horse knew the way home!

Stittsville Flea Market

Once upon a time the Stittsville Flea Market was the largest indoor-outdoor flea market in Eastern Ontario, and just fifteen minutes from Ottawa. Thousands of people would visit the market every Sunday (the only day it was open). Hundreds of thousands were deeply dismayed when the market closed in 2004, and maybe that's why more than 250,000 people ended up viewing this picture and leaving so many comments. One of our best posts ever!

Michelle: I always looked forward to going there as a kid!

Jesse: Hated that place as a kid. Got dragged there every Sunday.

Sue: It was a zoo!

Wendy: I think I can see my car!

Frank: I still can't find the car to my keys.

Janine: I loved going there! You never knew what you would find, and I sold homemade crafts for quite a nice profit.

Dorothy: Wasn't it Gibson's Flea Market back in the day?

Donna: Yes it was. My dad used to help John Gibson every Sunday and also with auctions.

Marc: "Just beyond the fringe," just like Dilawri's.

Douglas: I grew up spending lots of time there, where our family routinely sold baked goods, as well as handmade leather goods.

Melanie: My parents had an antiques booth outside. I used to hide in the furniture marked "do not open" to scare people … when they naturally opened it anyway.

Patti: I had my first job there when I was 14, selling donuts.

Selma: I worked there for many years at several "chip stands," and sometimes delivering tables to the different vendors. It paid well, and I met lots of interesting people! At the end of the day, as we punched out, manager Mr. Kavanagh would often give us a $20 — just because!

Justine: The Stittsville Flea Market was my backyard for 12 years. All the kids on my street (Neil Avenue) worked there, and I remember working the Beavertail stand at 15 years old. Very fond memories. Plus, I learned to drive in the parking lot, which was always completely empty Monday through Saturday!

Gail: I loved going there and really miss it. So many great vendors, fresh produce, handmade furniture, antiques … nothing else like it.

Marlene: I went there every Sunday, where I could decompress and visit with the vendors.

Nick: My best friend and I used to bike down there from Kanata to check out all the sweet stuff!

Dan: It was like the trip of a lifetime, coming from Lanark County.

Teresa: My hubby and I spent many a Sunday there wandering through the various stalls ... just loved it! Bought our gorgeous antique china cabinet and a magazine table there, among other treasures ...

Maria: I used to go all the time! Still have some of the jewelry I bought back in the '80s.

Dan: That's where we bought our "Cream Jeans."

Pat: And where else would we get our "Howicks" for so cheap!

Sharron: I used to work for Louie and would straighten up all the tall piles of pants.

Pat: We would go there rain or shine! Still have the first table we bought there as newlyweds, over 30 years ago!

Mel: It was a ritual every Sunday. Like going to church. I think every pirated eight-track in the world was sold there.

David: It was also a great place to get records.

Melanie: That and every novel known to man, not to mention

(National Capital Commission Map of Ottawa, 2002)

that indoor store with all the Pez and *Star Wars* stuff.

Josh: I still laugh about my pal who got an amazing deal on an "Alpine" car stereo. Then we went to install it. Once we squinted and read the face of it, what it really said was "Afine" ... hahaha!

Rick: When I first moved to Ottawa in 1985, this was a regular stop for me and anyone who was visiting. So much fun, so much food eaten, so much junk acquired!

Lee: It was a huge treat for me to get out there, which I could only do when my friends and I could scrape together enough money to pay someone's gas ... got a lot of cool stuff. Totally good times!

Ian: It was a big part of my childhood growing up. Of course, living in Stittsville at that time, and being a kid, there weren't a whole lot of options!

Max: So why did it close if it was so popular?

Cheryl: We had a booth there for ten years selling beeswax candles. Then they changed the law so that all stores could be open on Sundays (around 1992) and that eventually killed the flea market.

Anne: Unfortunately, more people than ever shop online. Sadly, they miss out on the human interaction. It was so cool bartering to get the right price.

Claudette: I'd forgotten about the bartering ...

Marc: I heard a story about how the land for the flea market was lost in a poker game ... no idea if that's true.

Patricia: It was lost in a poker game many years before it closed.

Mel: I believe it's true about the poker game, but that was many years ago, and not the reason it closed.

Jay: It's a good thing they made good use of that land ... oh wait they didn't.

Bob: It's starting to get developed.

Izzy: They're building a retirement home, and planning on building two apartment complexes.

Joan: I loved going there.

Art: I remember it well, and miss it just as much. Screw progress!

Veronica: I really miss it. We moved to Ottawa in 1990 and so enjoyed all the sights, sounds and smells of the great food out there. It sure improved Sunday afternoons for us and it was a real piece of Ottawa Valley living! Truly lost, but not forgotten!

FALL

Car Raffle at the Ex

One of the big features of the Ottawa Ex was the daily draw for a new car. Here's a Plymouth Valiant on top of a ticket booth, waiting for its lucky winner circa 1975.

Geoff: Did anyone ever actually win one of those cars, or was it just a midway scam?

Dave: I did, for one dollar in 1975.

Gilles: I remember when you won that car, Dave!

Dave: Same model as the picture, only brown. I felt like the luckiest guy alive.

Daniel: My first car was a 1975 Valiant, but with the 318 V8 instead of the Slant Six.

Glenn: Mine was the '75 Dodge Dart "Swinger." Pretty much the same car, and in this colour too.

Brian: A friend of mine owns a 1973 Fury given away at the Ex.

John: My friend Dan won a car there.

Dan: A 1980 Pontiac Sunbird. It was great, and certainly a step up from my Bobcat wagon with the fake wood on the side.

Vern: Mr. Glavin, my Latin teacher at Nepean High School (1957 to 1961) won a Plymouth.

Doug: My brother won a car in 1972.

David: My brother-in-law won a car at the Ex in 1946.

Aline: My grandmother won a car two years in a row. What are the chances?!

Kathie: My dad used to buy tickets for the car. Never won, though.

Cindy: My dad would listen to Rough Rider games on CFRA, waiting for them to announce the winner on a warm August night. I can still hear it.

Barry: I remember my father listening to the radio at 10:30 to see if his number was drawn ... you had to get back to Lansdowne Park within the hour to claim your car.

Vern: That's right, you had one hour to present yourself with the winning number.

Valerie: My father always bought tickets on the car. I remember those tense moments, waiting for the winning ticket to be drawn. Needless to say, he never won.

Doreen: My dad once had the second ticket drawn ... and then the winning ticket-owner showed up. Although my dad never drove in his life, winning a car might have inspired him!

Harry: They also gave away houses for a few years.

Chris: Cars were given away daily, but "tickets on the house" were only drawn on the last day of the Ex.

Peter: But houses and cars weren't all you could win. Those canopies on the upper left were the game stalls, where my favourite game was the dime-toss. My friends and I would come home with boxes of cheap glassware that always made my mom shudder.

Sandy: I spent a lot of time flipping dimes to try to win those glass goblets. As teens, we also played a lot of Crown and Anchor for a quarter a turn.

Orlando: I remember trying to win/rescue a budgie at the dime-throwing game. The dime had to land on a plate in front of all these tiny, noisy cages, each with a budgie or canary. Then there was the live mouse, with people betting on which hole he'd go into.

Paul: I once won a huge panda bear at the Ex by throwing two out of three ping-pong balls into goldfish bowls. Loved the Ex, the smells, the noise.

Tony: Don't forget the bingo tent!

Cathi: Right, the big tent just above the "bullet" in the picture. I used to play that with my mom, but for some reason or another this picture reminds me of daredevil motorcycle riders.

Chris: "Speedy" McNeish on the Wall of Death!

(Photo: Elizabeth G. Amey, shared by Brian Stants)

Night on the Towne

The Towne Cinema on Beechwood at Crichton in 1988, when it was still being run as a repertory film theatre. Despite its popularity, the cinema closed in 1989, when the same owners opened the Bytowne (get it?) on Rideau Street. Ironically, for all those who saw the *Rocky Horror Picture Show* there, perhaps, the old cinema is now a drugstore.

Gilles: Before it was the Towne, it was called the Linden Theatre and we could spend all afternoon there watching, usually, at least five movies.

Denis: I remember going to the Linden in the early 1960s, when my mother would give me a quarter. That got me in, and left enough for popcorn. My favourites were the horror movies. They often had two movies and somehow

we were always able to stay and watch them over again. I remember walking back home along McKay Street, scared as hell.

Philip: I went to a birthday party there in Grade One. Three horror hits! I had never seen anything remotely like it.

Jamie: Vincent Price! Scary as they come when you are ten!

Penelope: I saw *House of Wax* at the Linden and was terrified for a long time. Makes me shudder to think about it even now ...

Beth: Spent many, many Saturdays there watching cowboy movies.

(*Carleton Resolution*, 1988)

Jamie: *Jason and the Argonauts.*

Mickey: Audie Murphy, Tarzan, and the Bowery Boys. Three movies for a quarter and a dime for popcorn. My mom once took us to see the Elvis Presley movies, and I remember sitting upstairs with her in the smoking lounge.

Anne: I remember making my mom take me to see the Beatles' movies.

Barb: I recall my oldest sister Nancy McKenzie taking five of us to the Beatles movie *HELP*. We sat through it two times, and when it started for the third time they finally kicked us out.

Paul S: Saw *Life of Brian* on Good Friday at the Towne — with an apology note posted on the door saying the timing was not intentional.

Paul B: *Hair, Liquid Sky, Stop Making Sense, The Fourth Man, Koyaanisqatsi.* I can't begin to remember all of the amazing classics and screwed-up genre films I saw there in the late '80s. The Towne opened my eyes to the wonders of repertoire cinema …

Mike: This is where I saw *Spinal Tap* and *The Song Remains the Same*. There was smoking allowed back then — and not just cigarettes.

Bill: Saw *The Harder They Come* at the Towne, when I was expecting a Marx Brothers movie. For the first hour, I thought I was watching a Jamaican travelogue trailer. Combustibles were involved …

Paul L: Took my mom to see Pink Floyd's *The Wall* on rerun and everyone lit up the hash. The cops started running up and down the aisles. It looked exactly like a scene from the movie!

Bill: Saw *Rocky Horror Picture Show* (13 times, I believe). What a crazy place, always an adventure.

Brenda: *Quadrophenia, Kids are Alright, Song Remains the Same*, anything by Cheech and Chong. *Rocky Horror* over 100 times.

Steve: I can't even remember how many times I saw *Rocky Horror* there. Always a crazy bus ride from the Rideau Centre to the theatre with all the like-minded moviegoers (and their beverages) on OC Transpo! Wild nights!

Bill: So many nights lined up (stoned) to see *Rocky*. Over and over. What a blast that was.

Anita: The midnight showings? Partay!

Jean: The Towne is the only place I know that had sliding seats. I lost my virginity there, and saw *Rocky Horror Picture Show* the first time.

Rita: You know, the last show I saw at the Towne was … *Rocky Horror Picture Show*!

Patricia: Let's do the time warp again!

Glebe Collegiate

A weird curved version of Glebe Collegiate Institute on Glebe Avenue, taken for our ongoing series on local schools (and this was how Photoshop stitched it together, so what could I do?).

The school still has a "1922" on the front, for the year it was built. It also has the letters "OCI" – for Ottawa Collegiate Institute – because Glebe was originally an extension of what is now Lisgar. The schools have been rivals ever since!

Jaan: In 1922, there was only "The Collegiate Institute," administered by the Collegiate Institute Board. In a sense, all Ottawa high schools were branches of the Collegiate Institute until 1970, although different school sites took on separate names, of course.

Rachel: I never knew that! Calling it a "collegiate" makes more sense now.

Bryan: Interesting connection to Lisgar.

Jodi: Don't believe it. Clearly the person who posted this is a Lisgar alum!

J.E.: But we all know Glebe offered so much more to the students. Then again, I might be a tad biased.

Colin: I went to Glebe in the '60s and always thought Lisgar wanted to be us.

Eric: Lisgar wanted to be Ashbury! I don't recall thinking of Glebe at all in the 1980s.

Marg: Lisgar was and always will be better!

Andrew: With the exceptions of Reach for the Top, football and soccer.

Tanya: I went to both schools. There was always rivalry between Lisgar and Glebe for soccer and rugby. Lisgar took it in tennis, band and math.

Peggy: My mom went to Lisgar. She mentioned a rivalry with the marching bands.

Cheryl: My husband went to "Lisper!" GASP!

Tasha: Cheryl, how awful! My hubby was the drummer at Nepean (always had a soft spot for drummers).

Susan: My father went to Glebe, and my mom to Lisgar, so there must have been some fraternizing between student bodies.

Marg: Well, *their* bodies anyway ...

Wendy: Remember Glebe was only half of the building. For the

longest time, High School of Commerce was in the other half.

Judy: I didn't know Commerce shared the building. Interesting factoid!

James: The Ottawa High School of Commerce was attached to the west part of Glebe Collegiate Institute in 1929.

Beryl: I went to Commerce from 1965 to 1969. All 1,100 students moved to the new school on Rochester on Monday, April 17, 1967, Centennial Year.

Sharon: My mom went to Glebe when Commerce was there. I wonder if the actual building, looking so proud, had a positive effect on the students. No calling teachers by their first names. No pajamas worn to class. You did not hand in assignments late when it cost five marks a day, and if you only got 50 percent you FAILED. We all lived through it and went on to thrive in the real world. Without counselling ... or those stupid spin toys. So endeth my rant!

Michel: I almost decided to go to Commerce, one block from home, but who wanted to study data processing? What kind of future is there in a machine that counts numbers at the speed of light! Rather play in the Glebe bands!

Cheryl: I still have the album that the Senior and Stage Bands made as a fundraiser for the trip to England. The school song is there and I play the MP3 more than you might imagine!

Tasha: I remember when we made that record at CJOH. It would have been in 1974, maybe in the Fall? The band trip was March 1975 (my last year). Man, that was fun!

Liz: Is it embarrassing to say that I can still sing most of the songs?

Kristanne: Two bits, four bits ....

Bill: Six bits, a dollar. Everyone for Glebe, stand up and holler!

(Lost Ottawa)

Parkwood Hills

September 22, 2017: likes 259, 46 shares, 43 comments, 20,080 reached

Shared by Charlie Senack, here's the Mulvagh family facing west on what is now Meadowlands Drive in Parkwood Hills, farm buildings behind them on the hilltop. So now you know how Parkwood Hills and Meadowlands got their names, not to mention Mulvagh Avenue nearby — the whole neighbourhood was once farmland.

Now? The only wide-open spaces are in the parking lots of the malls along Merivale!

Charlie: The Mulvagh farm stretched from Meadowlands to Fisher, and along Merivale from the present location of the Independent Grocer to Emerald Plaza. Next was the Stewart farm, then the Borden Dairy farm, where Viewmount is today.

Ann: Just to the left of this photo, there is a hilly field and trail behind the mall. If you love the songs of insects, this is the best place in Ottawa to hear them. Miss the neighbourhood!

Robb: We used to ski down that hill.

Susan: We used to go tobogganing there.

(Charlie Senack)

Cheryl: I now live on Chesterton Drive. It's hard to imagine Parkwood Hills as farmland.

Philip: I live on Kilmory, not far away from the scene of this picture. Some of the original owners here still talk about the early 1960s when there were cows on the other side of the street.

Mary: My family was one of the original families to move into Parkwood Hills in the fall of 1961. At the time, Meadowlands, Newberry, and Tiverton all stopped at the bottom of the hill. We would pet Mr. Mulvagh's horses at recess when Parkwood Hills Public School first opened.

Dave: There were cows and horses in this field until the mid-1960s. We certainly had cows and horses behind our house on Argue Drive in Carleton Heights.

Karen: Dave, I remember the horses and cows in the field behind our house, as well as the raspberry bushes along the fence.

Michelle: My parents bought 19 Chesterton Drive. There were cows across the street from our house in 1966.

Dave: My parent's backyard on Argue Drive is now Four Seasons Drive. When I was a kid we used to help Harry Leiken bale his hay along the Borden Side Road over to Fisher Avenue.

Elaine: We lived at 5 Mulvagh Street. I remember the farmhouse at Chesterton and Mulvagh and the empty barn across Meadowlands.

Dave: After their original barn burnt down, Chesterton Towers was built on the site. I believe their homestead at the corner of Chesterton is now a church.

Charlie: Their homestead was right where the new expansion of Parkwood Presbyterian is now, but no barns or houses burned down. The house was torn down for the expansion of the church only a few years ago.

Rob: I grew up on Inverness and recall a huge fire in the mid-1960s. We could see the smoke from our place and our dad drove us up to see what was happening.

Charlie: That must have been the barn on the Stewart farm, right next to the Mulvagh farm, where Chesterton Towers is.

Dave: Oh right, the barn that overlooked the back of Kmart. The story I heard was that a few guys were trying to impress the girls by playing a game of "I dare you" with matches. They'd start a fire, then stamp it out. One of the girls got scared and opened the barn door to leave. A gust of wind fed the flames. All ran away safely.

Ann: And you were one of those boys with the matches, right?

Dave: No, no, no ... I watched the fire through binoculars on the roof of my parents house. I just heard about it from the gang out front of Kmart the next day!

Bells Corners

October 3, 2017: 584 likes, 159 shares, 117 comments, 41,953 reached

Here we are in Bells Corners, looking west along Robertson Road towards Moodie, circa 1980. You can see the Bel-Air Motel, Midas Muffler, Consumer's Distributing and McDonald's. Strip commercial at it's finest!

These were the days when Bells Corners was renowned for its ugliness and — just to emphasize the point — the photographer used a telephoto lens to compress the distance and enhance the suburban splendour.

Sharon: Sign, sign, everywhere a sign, ugh ...

Bram: With a long lens, you can make any place look like a Las Vegas wasteland.

Ron: Yes, it is amazing what the foreshortening from the telephoto lens does. It must be at least 500 metres from the Bel-Air to the McDonald's, but it looks a lot closer in the photo.

Adam: It really was quite ugly. So ugly people would often say, "we don't want our neighbourhood to become another Bells Corners." Like Merivale Road, for example?

Louise: I lived in Bells Corner in the 1980s. We used to call it Junk Food Alley. McDonald's, Burger King, Wendy's, Kentucky Fried Chicken.

Erma: You forgot Harvey's and all the pizza places.

Marilyn: I remember Harvey's when it was small and had a window and you ate at picnic tables outside.

John: I worked at the Burger King in the late '70s when I was in high school.

Peter: I worked at the McDonald's at the same time.

Jessica: When I was a kid, the McDonald's there still had the old orange, yellow, and brown decor. There were those seats near the bathroom with the conveyor belt that delivered food to the drive-thru. Plus the caboose, where I had my sixth birthday party!

Ian: I believe Bells Corners had one of the earliest Tim Horton's in the Ottawa area.

Roger: The first Tim's in Ottawa was the one in the plaza at Bank near Walkley, across from the GM dealership.

Robert: Lived right behind Tim Horton's in Bells Corners from 1981-1995. The fresh donut smells never got old!

Sarah: At some point Bells Corners had the only Arby's anywhere near Ottawa.

Perry: Frank Vetere's predated the Arby's in that building.

Colleen: There was Frank Vetere's, Ponderosa, Mother's ... the good old days!

Warren: Mother's was great ... it became Hurley's?

Colleen: I wanna say yes, but I'm not entirely sure. I thought Mother's was in the building that eventually became the Keg.

Tom: The Keg is still there at the corner of Robertson. Mother's was in its own building.

Cam: Wasn't Mother's once the Country Bar Lounge in the corner of the Kmart parking lot? Corkscrew was in the building that later became the Vox lounge.

Jeff: And before that Chi Chi's, and before that Red Lobster.

Tom: Al's Steakhouse was at the intersection of Old Richmond Road and Robertson, with Fat Albert's nearby.

Christine: When I arrived in Canada in 1978, I drove through Bells Corners, and had my first Canadian pizza at Fat Albert's. Yum! The next day I discovered the Richmond Bakery!

Ryan: Bells Corners sucks now. It used to be so much better. There was Pizza Hut, Quickee, Foody Goody ...

Tom: Holy crap. Foody Goody!!!

Robert: Foody Goody was Bells Corners for me ....

Joanne: The most disgusting Chinese food buffet ever! It was a blessing when it closed.

Aaron: Barely food ... and light-years from good!

Woolworths Lunch Counter

Ottawa had quite a few downtown department stores back in the day, and it seems like every single one of them had a lunch counter. In honour of that ancient tradition, we posted this promo shot of the brand new lunch counter at Woolworths on Sparks Street, taken for opening day in 1941.

No Photoshop in those days, but the picture does make it look like the counter stretched all the way from Sparks Street to Queen!

Terry: Now, THAT is a lunch counter! I saw an *Ottawa Journal* article that claimed the Woolworths on Sparks Street had the longest straight-line counter in Canada, at 180 feet.

Anne: From the days when you could just take a seat and wait for service.

Debbie: When people weren't in such a rush all the time.

Marnie: Food was affordable and you got to talk to your neighbour at the counter. I loved those lunch counters.

Jane: I had lunch there most weekdays in the late 1950s and early 1960s.

Alida: I sat in those chairs and remember the food was very good!

Bev: I worked across from Woolworths on Sparks Street. We went for lunch every day and always sat at the counter. The food was always good.

Jeanie: I used to sneak down there every now and then, when I worked at Met Life. Did anyone have a ketchup smear on the policies I was typing?

Betty: Brings back memories of my mother-in-law and I and our Saturday shopping trips which would always end with a trip to Woolworths and a banana split. Miss you Mom!

Kate: My gramma used to don a girdle (a tortuous feat), put on one of her best hats, then take me downtown on the #2 bus to do a little shopping and have lunch at the Woolworths (or Ogilvy's) counter. Grilled cheese sandwiches, cherry cheesecake, and time with my grandmother — priceless!

Blair: Every year on my birthday, my big sister would take me by bus to see the Changing of the Guard, followed by a trip to Woolworths for a Coke and chips (as we called French fries then).

Trish: My mom, sister and I went there often. Mom would order two banana splits and three Cokes. My sister and I would share one of the splits and think we were pretty special.

Gillian: I sat there on many a Saturday enjoying a banana split. If your receipt had a red star, your split was free. If not, I recall it cost 39 cents.

Nancy: Used to go for the egg-salad sandwich.

Bruce: How about that coffee for a nickel!

Doreen: Either hot chicken, turkey, beef or hamburger sandwiches, with peas and carrots, or coleslaw and fries with gravy. It was so darn good. Not even the finest steakhouse dinner can erase the pleasant memories.

Andre: Not too many restaurants even offer hot sandwiches anymore. How does a hot sandwich go out of style?

Heather: Took the bus from Manor Park. Mum would treat us to club sandwiches with fancy toothpicks.

John: Remember the club sandwiches with potato chips in the middle?

Gisele: They had the apple dumplings with vanilla sauce.

Wendy: Oh, those apple dumplings, with a custard sauce to die for. The beginning of my sweet tooth.

Gail: French fries, a chocolate sundae with real ice cream and spinning around on those chairs.

Robert: Milkshakes sliding down the counter. Wonder who invented curling?

Yvan: These counters were designed for you to stay and relax. Nowadays eateries are designed for you to sit and go as fast as possible.

Roisin: You would think that lunch counters would be more popular than ever ... now that we all have our phones for lunch dates!

(City of Ottawa Archives CA024215)

The Mayfair Theatre

October 20, 2017: 426 likes, 81 shares, 64 comments, 25,917 reached

The Mayfair Theatre in May of 1977, during the cinema's "dark" period, when it was probably a good idea to step into Mannie's Confectionary, or drop into Patty's Place for a beer, to wait until it was finally dark and you could sneak into your porno movie without being seen by your neighbours!

Liz: Vern's V.I.P. is next door!

Samantha: So cool to see this because Vern and Marcella are my grandparents.

Jayson: I used to go to Vern's when I was a little boy and our family owned the stretch of businesses across the street.

Andy: My first haircut was at Vern's V.I.P. in 1974.

Alex: I used to go to Mannie's for penny candy.

Anne: I remember stopping at Mannie's for penny candy before going to the movies.

Jennifer: When I went there as a kid, the confectionary was still called Watts.

Jean: My Uncle!

(City of Ottawa Archives CA018896)

Jennifer: We got an allowance of 35 cents per week. Five cents for the bus from Heron Road to the Mayfair, ten cents for candy at Watts, fifteen cents to get in, and five cents to get back home.

Connie: Saturdays in the 1950s, my mom would send us to the Mayfair with 25 cents which covered entry and snacks for the double features and cartoons.

Janice: Saturday matinees! Balcony seats and two bad kids squirting wet popcorn kernels down onto the people on the main floor!

Dianne: I grew up on Sunnyside and went to the Mayfair every Saturday. There was a glass booth at an angle where you bought your ticket for 25 cents. I remember them showing newsreels between the movies in which they spoke of "guerrillas." As an 11-year-old, I thought they were referring to the animals, not the soldiers!

Barb: My husband took me there on our first date in 1958, and many times later after that. Glad to hear it's still there.

Sandria: I went there in my early teens, when most of my friends lived in that area. My sisters caught me kissing my boyfriend and teased me forever!

Sheila: Used to go in the 1980s. Loved the seats. First row in the balcony. Lots of extra leg room.

Stephen: I spent many an evening there in the back rows, where you could smoke.

Glenn: I remember being able to smoke in the upper section for a few years in the late 1970s.

Jim: The first movie I ever saw was *The Lady and the Tramp* at the Mayfair. It was 35 cents to get in, five cents for a drink, and ten cents for that pink popcorn in a box.

Pamela: First movie for me was *The Sound of Music* at the Mayfair when I was ten years old.

Henry: I remember seeing my first Hitchcock movies there. A double bill of *Spellbound* and *North by Northwest*.

Su: I went to the Mayfair as a kid. It was magical. I especially remember seeing *Batman* with all those captions. Biff, Baff, Pow!

Donna: I saw the *Exorcist* here.

Linda: Does anyone remember the scary lady!?

Dianne: I remember two sisters with beehive hairdos who were pretty strict. They would walk up and down the aisle with a flashlight making sure no one was kissing or smoking.

Linda: The scary lady yelled at my brother Bruce once, then kicked him out. He was just sitting and laughing. I felt so sad for him.

Eric: Was that Mrs. Armstrong ?

John: Mrs. Robinson.

Eric: That seemed too obvious.

Raiding the Chez Henri

Ottawa has its own bars, of course, but we all know where the real drinking took place in times gone by — across the river in Hull where the Chez Henri was just one of several places you could drink for hours after the good folks of Ottawa had gone to bed.

If you were lucky, or underage, you might get the added thrill of a ride in the paddy wagon, like these patrons of the Chez Henri in the 1970s.

Peter: That looks like my friend Ricky in line.

Mark: It does looks like him, waiting his turn to get in the wagon.

Kim: When I saw this, I wondered if I was being loaded into that van. Maybe just "a little" too early.

Paul: I'm in the van already.

Denis: I'm on the right in this photo, with the suede coat with white cuffs and collar. My girlfriend is beside me. We didn't get to ride the paddy wagon that night — but we are still together!

Brenna: This is hilarious, yet so accurate for what the police used to do on the Strip into the late 1990s.

John: Were they raiding for prostitution?

Deborah: Underage drinkers.

Jaan: And drugs.

Valerie: I never went to Chez Henri, but I've been to the Ottawa House, Standish Hall, the Chaud, upstairs and down (aka "the Pit"), as well as the Glenlea, and even once to the really shady Interprovincial Hotel (now that was quite the experience).

Terry: I got an awful shock running out the back door of the Interprovincial as cops came in the front — it was like a 30-foot drop to the ground beside the bridge. Thankfully, the snow softened the stop. Yes, I was underage …

Valerie: The first time I went to the Ottawa House, I was 14!

Patricia: I hung out at all those wonderful places in Hull and Aylmer like the Chamberlain and the Chaud. Met my future husband at the Chamberlain in 1968. Still married!

George: Back in the 1960s, my 20-year-old father and his dad would go to the Chez Henri. It was known for its ladies of the night. My father was known for his high libido. My grandfather would take all my dad's money, just in case.

Paul: I worked at the new city hall on Green Island from 1958-1959, and would slip over to the Chez Henri on Tuesday evenings to wait until it was

(City of Ottawa Archives CA024971)

time to bowl. The "ladies" were always active and we could see them come and go, even during the short time we were there. The saying was "low dollars on the left" and "high dollars on the right." Fun times when you are 19 years old.

Lisa: My best memory of the Chez is of a night with my friend Dayna, when we were trying to ditch this football player, only to have him keep popping up next to us. Then we had to sneak him back into his dorm.

Dayna: Sneaking into a dorm, trying to smuggle a huge (drunk) football player into his room undetected. Thank goodness they didn't have security cameras everywhere back then!

Maureen: I remember being herded into the paddy wagon and brought to the cop-shop in Hull for underage drinking. We had our IDs, but they just wouldn't check them until we got to the police station, where we were then stranded, with no ride back to Ottawa or the bar. My first and only time in a paddy wagon!

Julie: You and I had to take the bus, but we were back within the hour, dancing to the MRQ!

Chelsea: Julie, you were brought to a police station in a paddy wagon?

Julie: Not my fault. I have always been young looking!

Minted Grape

November 5, 2018: 262 likes, 26 shares, 129 comments, 21,322 reached

You never know what you'll find in your old Ottawa house, but do check the vents. That's where Marwane Salibi found this can of Pure Spring Minted Grape soda pop.

What's in a name? They call it "soda" in the U.S., but "pop" where I grew up in B.C. It's "soda pop" for some, and "soft drinks" for others — but Minted Grape? I'm not sure I've ever heard of that one.

Andrew: Minted Grape! That's the holy grail of pop!

Gordon: Since there's metric on the can, it must be from the mid-1970s, and it's one rare can because those ones were so hard to open you often had to use a pen, or something hard, and if you did it the wrong way, well, you would get sprayed. And grape stains badly!

Maureen: Love Minted Grape! Used to be a staple in the vending machines at Carleton in the early 1980s.

Elizabeth: We had Minted Grape in our high-school vending machine at Thomas More High School. Sometimes, no matter what button you pushed, you got back Minted Grape *and* your change!

Pierre: Minted Grape was the best POP ever.

Ken: Wait, we say pop? I only ever said soft drink, I believe …

Lesley: I grew up saying pop, but started calling it soda as I got older.

Steve: I always said soft drink!

Brian: Agree. Soft drink.

Glenn: We always said soft drink too. Is this an Ottawa thing?

Steve: Could be!

Brian: My cousins say pop up in the Soo.

Nancy: I'm from Ontario and have always called them sodas (as in cream soda) or soft drinks, but my partner from Nova Scotia calls them pop.

Thomas: I'm from the east coast, but grew up in Regina and Winnipeg. My friends, family and I all pretty much used the term pop.

Joan: Soft drinks.

Gordon: Soft drinks is the term that became popular in the 1930s, when they used mixers to cut the hard taste of home-made booze. So you had Hard Drinks = Bathtub Gin, and Soft Drinks = Tonic Water.

Chris: I miss Pure Spring and all their flavours.

Nancy: Minted Grape and Honee Orange were my faves.

Gavin: Minted Grape was the best grape pop ever made. I also remember Cuban Cola as being very good.

Lynn: Right up there with Pure Spring Cream Soda.

Tony: The rarest is Spruce Beer. A very acquired taste, sort of like Buckley's Mixture.

David: Spruce Beer is horrible. Tastes like tree sap.

Gordon: It IS tree sap!

JP: Carbonated turpentine.

Gordon: Actually ... that is a very accurate description!

Jace: I LIKED the Spruce Beer!

Andrea: Our dad was the manager of Pure Spring in Ontario for 19 years, so we drank a lot of soft drinks. My favourite was called Grand Slam. Yum.

Wendy: They tested all kinds of flavours, including pineapple.

(Shared by Marwane Salibi)

Diego: Around 1967 they even made a chocolate soda. That didn't last long.

John: But Pure Spring's Ginger Ale was the best ever.

David: It was the Goldie Locks of ginger ales. Not too dry and not too sweet. Just right. Never heard of Minted Grape, though!

Fran: As children in Ottawa in the 1950s, the only brand of pop my brothers and I were ever allowed (and that rarely) was Pure Spring. No Coke for us. Minted Grape was my fave!

Carol: I had forgotten Minted Grape, but after seeing it again I can almost taste it.

Jeff: Bring back Minted Grape!

Max: Don't drink it, Marwane. We might need it.

Marwane: Unfortunately, it was already open ...

115

On the Merivale Road

Justin S. Campbell shared this picture of Merivale Road looking south from Meadowlands in October of 1980. It confirmed our suspicions ... that driving on Merivale has always been terrible!

Adam: So traffic in that section of Merivale was as bad in 1980 as it is today?

Shirley: Bumper to bumper ... then and now!

Shaun: Under construction ... then and now!

Blaine: Just as ugly ... then and now! An example of "progress" gone completely wrong.

Ken: Merivale Road has always had awful traffic problems. I can't figure out why ... it must be badly engineered or something.

Charles: Ha, such fun! When Merivale Mall opened, it seemed it was the very next day that they started to widen Merivale Road. For several years I had no trouble keeping even with the traffic on my evening walks down Merivale to the mall. If I needed to take the car, I used the back roads.

Chrissy: I lived in the area in the 1990s. No issues then.

Todd: No issues? Traffic along that stretch of Merivale has been rated as

(Larry McDougall, *Ottawa Citizen*.)

some of the worst in the entire province since the late 1980s. I myself was rear-ended twice in front of Merivale Mall, and hit by a car while on my bike. Merivale Road keeps trying to kill me! But I'm a fighter. Haha!

Ted: People! That's just the line-up for the beer store.

Hartley: I bought my first underage 12-pack at that beer store, nervous as hell.

Shon: Spent Friday night sitting around the corner at that beer store, waiting for some nice guy to buy us beer. We would hand him a pile of change, back when five dollars would get you a pack of smokes and a six-pack. Then we would go to the bushes beside Merivale High School and drink, or to Hog's Back.

Linda: That Brewer's Retail store was my dad's weekly stop, so we also ordered from Gow's for many years. Good memories, growing up in Nepean!

Gail: We often used to ride our bikes to Gow's for fries in the evening ... something to do. Sit on the dirty curb, eat them, then bike off again. Behind the strip mall was just fields and a creek ... and very dark at night.

Keith: Gow's had awesome fries.

Cindy: Gow's had cheap smokes.

Faith: Gow's had the best open-ended egg rolls. I used to see the ladies sitting in the back making them.

Mats:. Hung out nights at that mall. Gow's egg rolls were fantastic, but what a boring place. Lot of teeny-bop smooching behind Zellers, though.

Christine: Back in high school, when my family lived on Bowhill right behind this plaza, we would hang out and smoke at that McDonald's up the road.

Linda: Walked to that McDonald's every chance I got as a youngster.

Mats: What many don't know is that the Merivale McDonald's was Ottawa's first. I used to skip classes at Merivale High to go there. Hamburgers were 20 cents, fries 15 cents, and a drink 10 cents. The whole menu was four or five items. Not even Big Macs.

Jamie: They eventually did get Big Macs in the mid-to-late 1970s. I remember them having a height chart that said at one point on the scale: "You're big enough for a Big Mac." And so, sure enough, the next time I went to McDonald's that's what I ordered.

Paul: I worked at the Merivale McDonald's from 1981 to 1985. Best group of people I ever met.

Janet: Met my husband at that McDonald's.

Mike: I was the head chef at McDonald's in the late 1970s.

Wendy: "Chef" and "McDonald's" in the same sentence?

Mike: Easy now!

Scott Street in Winter

Looking east down Scott Street toward downtown Ottawa in the 1960s, when Tunney's Pasture on the left was still, well, mostly pasture.

Wrote Tino LaFratta, who shared this photo: "This picture was taken around 1960 near Scott Street and Gilchrist Avenue, beside the CPR tracks where the Transitway is now. That's Scott Street to the right of the poles and my house is the white one on the right. The building on the left was already gone when I grew up."

Marty: I grew up on Caroline near Scott in the 1950s and '60s. That building on the left was at the northeast corner of Smirle and Scott. It was an axe factory.

Brian: Both my grandmother and aunt lived on Smirle Avenue right by Scott Street. I see my aunt's small white bungalow, with a white garage in front of it, across from the "Lizzie Borden Axe Factory." I can also see the top of my grandmother's two-storey house across the street. Milk was delivered in bottles by horse-drawn cart. Steam trains ran by and if you waved at the train, the engineer would wave back and blow the whistle. We used to walk through Tunney's Pasture down to the river, and that's where I learned to skip stones.

Sherree: We rented a place on Carleton Street, north of Scott around 1963. I was three years old and my mum would take me to the river on outings.

Rick: Anyone remember the tracks crossing Holland at Scott Street, and the old liquor store?

Don: My old house is just out of view, but still standing, and I remember having to walk to St. François School, then back home for lunch, then back to school and home again. But sometimes we had to wait for the train to cross Scott Street at "Holland Cross" to the Beach Foundry.

Jim: And I used to go into that liquor store with my dad. It was the old-style setup where you had to write what you wanted on the piece of paper and somebody would go in the back and bring it out to you.

Don: There were many car accidents at that corner. We had many bloody people come to our house to use the phone. Half of my dad's tools were always to be found on our front lawn.

Tino: I remember running almost daily to that corner to check out the accidents.

Patrick: The level crossings along Scott Street were all extremely dangerous. There were so many fatal accidents, usually involving motorists who attempted to "race" the trains at the various cross streets.

Don: I guess those CPR tracks were removed around 1967 and now new tracks will be placed there for the LRC. What goes around, comes around!

Kristan: The railway tracks were largely still there until they built the Transitway, especially at major road crossings where the rails were sunk in the pavement (at Churchill, for example). I remember driving over them in the late 1970s, looking down the line and asking my parents when the train was coming.

Chantal: I grew up at the corner of Carruthers and Stonehurst. Those tracks were our playground, until we had to move in 1983. That's when our house was purchased and demolished to build the Transitway.

Anne: We used to play on those tracks for hours … putting down pennies, rocks and anything else we could find. Then we would wait for the trains to squash it. I lived near the corner of Scott and Island Park Drive in the 1960s. I doubt our parents even knew we were playing there. Hahaha!

(Shared by Tino LaFratta)

Shortt's Confectionary

One of our big themes of 2017 was corner stores, and one of our biggest stories of the year featured this 1966 picture of Shortt's Confectionery, located at 504 Hilson Avenue on the corner of Iona in Westboro.

A little later, Shortt's became Frangioni's, which then became Hilson Confectionery, owned by the Spasojevic family. Kids of all ages remember the store with an amazing fondness.

Michael: Dorothy Shortt was head cashier at the Dominion Store at Kirkwood and Carling (not too far away from Hilson). She quit that job to take over the store. All the kids from Hilson Public and St. George's Catholic would stop there to buy this and that. She was a very kind person.

Linda: Those little corner stores were always terrific. I can still smell the Double Bubble.

Cindy: This was my childhood corner store, where I spent my weekly allowance of 25 cents on the best penny candy ever!

Steven: Passed by it four times a day on my way to and from Hilson Public. No eating lunch at school then. Bought many a jaw-breaker, rockets, candy cigarettes, and assorted other favs. Yum!

Jo: For five cents I could get 25 candies, including sour cherries, black balls, and all kinds of great things on my way back to St. George's after lunch at home in the early 1960s.

Miguel: I remember cap guns and Popeye candy sticks!

Denise: I would stop by to get freezies after swimming in the pool at Iona Park.

Jean: My mom used to send me there to buy packs of cigarettes for her. Buckinghams with no filters, wow! I use to get bags of candy for a nickel or a dime, three for a penny. I remember the woman was so nice she once gave me a chocolate bar right before I was having my tonsils out so I could have a treat later.

Wayne: That's where I got caught buying a pack of smokes by my dad in 1966. He wasn't very happy!

Beth: We used to stop in after school in the mid-1980s for penny candy. My Swedish Berry addiction started there!

Michael: I can still see the owner of Frangioni's behind the glass, picking out those Swedish Berries.

Laurie: It was later owned by the Spasojevics. They had three daughters and I went to school with Zel and Dragana.

Diana: Our family bought the place in 1979. I'm the oldest of the three daughters who worked in the store every day. Zel is the middle, and Dragana is the youngest. Our parents built out the house and modernized it, but running a store like that means a lot of open hours and profitability was really hurt when the new and large supermarkets opened very close by. In 2002, they decided to convert the store into another form of income and created a duplex instead.

Glen: Your mom and dad were the best! Always treated the neighbourhood kids like royalty.

Kevin: I somehow remember this store as being owned by a man named "Dragonfly." That can't be right!

Zel: My dad's name was Dragomir, but Dragonfly is brilliant, too! It was a hoot working there as young girls. I can still hear the store bell ring, and the sweet smell of the candy counter, over which my dad put a glass top to keep fingers from contaminating the Jujubes, and also thwart a few sticky fingers from some of the kids in the hood!

Janet: Drago was a fixture behind the counter, and we all called him Mr. Spacojevic. Thanks for the memories!

Dragana: It's amazing how this one little place holds so many memories for so many people.

The Rideau Street Shelters

Saturday Shopping in downtown Ottawa in 1984, not long after the opening of the Rideau Centre. At the time, Rideau Street was its own transitway, with no cars allowed. They still had the two skywalks (now there's only one), and they still had the (in)famous bus shelters.

Wendy: I remember the crazy covered bus shelters down Rideau Street! Super-sketchy at night!

Marie-Aline: One of those "unintended consequences" scenarios. I worked at the Rideau Centre at the time, and the shelters just seemed to make the area less safe and deter shoppers.

Jeff: In the 1980s those shelters were great — for kids, panhandlers, and anyone looking to commit a crime! We could hang out in the dead of winter with the heaters on all day, smoke a little and drink a little, usually in front of Rock Junction. Seldom was there a police officer on foot on Rideau.

Mickey: The shelters were great for the first summer and winter. Then the

(Photo: Boris Spremo. Toronto Public Library, TSPA-0107397)

aggressive bums, panhandlers, and assorted lowlifes moved in. They could have been managed by an effective police foot patrol (even an auxiliary presence would have done the trick), but the city ruined it with deliberate political interference ...

Michael K: I agree. My hash business really went down the tubes when the city brought back beat cops in the market in the late 1990s!

Mike M: Those bus shelters were a nice idea on the drawing board. Practically, they were a disaster. At night, they created a great shelter for the homeless and quite a few of them used it as toilet space as well. Not one of the city's better ideas. I think it helped the decline of Rideau Street as a shopping mecca, and it still hasn't fully recovered.

Geoff: Rideau Street as a shopping destination began a boom at that time that still continues — the Rideau Centre is vastly busier than the rest of the street ever was.

Henry: I remember the artist's conception for the shelters looked really cool, but often you can't tell until it's too late that concept and reality are in different directions. I do give the city credit for trying something new for the times.

Bruce: Ottawa trying to make a preemptive move into the 21st century! It failed at the time, but today I think would be a great move in speeding up the much delayed transit system!

Andrew: Funny, this old set-up looks infinitely better than the way it does in 2017!

Amanda: Definitely beats the trash-can look it has now.

Nancy: Well, the Rideau bus shelters are the Crystal Gardens in Perth now. They were removed because the so-called drunks would sleep in them, but Rideau Street actually looked good back then. Now it's a jungle of tattoo parlours and filthy sidewalks. Sigh for the good old days.

Shannon: The Crystal Palace in Perth was made from the bus shelters?

Kevin: I remember seeing those when I visited Perth! I had no idea!

Philip: They were re-assembled beside the Tay Canal Basin and are now used for the farmers' market, concerts, dances, wedding receptions and a whole range of civic functions. As the Crystal Palace they're humming. They just needed to find their true purpose!

Eric: The shelters look quite good in Perth, but the whole Rideau Street design was a mess.

Chantal: A dark moment in Rideau Street history.

Ted: A ghastly miscalculation. You can have a vibrant shopping district or a bus mega-station, but not both.

Stephen: It looks so pristine in the photo. But we all remember the smell!

Michael Q: I can smell it as if it were yesterday.

Taking the "A" Train

Taking the "A" train through downtown Ottawa in the mid-1950s … and this really is the "A" car, about to turn right onto Queen Street and clickety-clack its way out to Britannia Park.

Peeking up over the car is the Lord Elgin Hotel. On the right is a series of buildings that would be replaced in the 1960s with the British High Commission and the (already lost) Lorne Building.

Kij: My father drove the Britannia streetcar when he first started working for the Ottawa Transportation Commission.

Kathy: My grandfather was a conductor on the Britannia Line.

Bruce: The Britannia Line was the last to go in 1959 when the streetcars were finished. I was operator #573 at that time. It was a big mistake to do away with them.

Janet: My cousin and I used to play on the old streetcars in the Britannia streetcar graveyard. We thought we were riding in grand style. What a time we had!

Trish: Our family used to take this trolley on a Saturday for a day of picnicking and swimming at Britannia Park. The ride was half the fun when you were little!

Paul: I wonder if the ride was smooth, compared to a bus?

Michael: Yes! Smooth ride with a little bit of sweet rock and roll, especially on the trip to and from Britannia!

Louise: I rode the streetcar almost every day to school, then to work, and then to Britannia on weekends. It was great fun, loved it.

Bob: I rode on this line to play gigs in the 1950s at a night spot in Britannia called the Ranch House. Left my saxophone under the seat of the streetcar one night. Recovered it next day in their barn.

Darlene: My dad and I rode this line from downtown to the west end when I was a kid.

Diane: As a kid, I remember taking the streetcar from Byron and Hilson Avenue on Fridays, meeting my parents at the Diamond Bar-B-Q for supper, then going to a Disney movie at the Regent or Capitol Theatre.

Judi: How I loved going downtown with my mom on the streetcar! It was such a treat to go to Murphy Gamble's or Freiman's.

Dianne: One of my most vivid memories as a child is riding this streetcar to Ogilvy's downtown with my mother.

Sue: I can remember streetcars toodling along Bank Street. Miss them.

Penny: If you lived in Sandy Hill in the 1950s, the streetcar came eastward down Rideau, went around down Charlotte and then west on Laurier. If you missed your car on Rideau, you could run through Lovers Lane, as it was called, and catch the car on Laurier instead.

Claire: I loved using the streetcars. The drivers knew who should be getting on at any given stop in the morning. If you weren't there they would advance a little to see if you were coming down the street and wait for you. I was sorry to see them go. Buses are not the same.

Marilyn: I liked the streetcar better than the buses.

Michelle: They should make all of downtown car-free and go back to streetcars. The tourist draw alone would be great. Give downtown some character!

Griffin: I don't know if car-free is a good idea for Ottawa, but a Sparks Street streetcar would sure be cool to have.

Wayne: Sad shame that they decided to take the whole streetcar system out in the first place. They weren't thinking ahead.

Neil: Please bring back the electric trolley!

Steve: Just a reminder .... the streetcars lost money. The first year the new OTC made money was the year after the streetcars were scrapped.

(Source Unknown)

125

Cats on the Hill

One of Ottawa's most endearing features in years gone by was the cat sanctuary on Parliament Hill. Here's a photo of the sanctuary in the summer of 2001, shared by volunteer Klaus Gerken, who helped take care of the cats for several years.

Started in the 1970s by Irene Desormeaux, the sanctuary was run from 1987 to 2008 by René Chartrand, with the help of numerous volunteers. It was kept going under the leadership of Brian Caines until January of 2013, when the last of the cats had either died or been adopted.

Jean: It was my great-grandmother Irene Desormeaux who started to take care of these cats. When she passed away her friend René Chartrand continued to take care of them.

Klaus: I have photographs of Irene on the Cats of Parliament Hill Memorial Facebook page. I myself spent seven years doing the weekend and holiday shift, helping René care for the cats, and I will always keep the memories alive through the blog and Facebook pages. These were not just René's or my cats, but Canada's cats. They belonged to all of us ... or maybe we belonged to them.

Marie: The cat sanctuary was the absolute best thing about the Hill and an obvious place to take anyone from out of town. It was quirky Canada at its best to not only have this delightfully ramshackle sanctuary, but also to have it right on the doorstep of Parliament.

Chris: It was always so heart-warming to have one of those older cats come up and sit in your lap though you'd never met before. I miss it, and think of it often.

Mangie: I'll always treasure the time spent with Fluffy, Blackie, Bebe, and the big orange boy purring on my lap!

Klaus: That would be Brownie.

Dee: A few days after moving solo from the Maritimes to Ottawa, I decided to go for a walk. Setting out, I was uneasy, because the highlights of life in my new hometown to that point were: an airport taxi driver who wanted to put my cats in the trunk, a skinhead with a Bowie knife, and local company employees who were angry that I was ever brought in. After walking for quite awhile I encountered the cat sanctuary. I was so impressed that the people of Ottawa cared for the colony. Right there on the spot, I decided maybe Ottawa

wasn't so bad and that maybe, just maybe, things would work out. Over 25 years and a career change later — I'm still here!

Edmund: My late wife and I used to take food up for René and the cats.

Suzanne: I recall spending my lunch hour petting the cats. Memories!

Souly: That was my favourite thing to go see when I was younger. It was the best thing about Parliament Hill.

Jim: The cats of Parliament Hill were always a "must see" highlight of any visits by out-of-towners, or doing the local tourist thing with family and friends.

Anne: We always took our visitors there! Miss it!

Klaus: My favourite story has always been the time a group of Japanese tourists came to see the cats. The tour director asked if there was anything else to see on the Hill. When I mentioned Centre Block and other sites ... they all piled back on the bus and left!

Barbara: Cats weren't the only animals that you and René looked after. Raccoons and squirrels, too. You and René were the kindest people. Miss the cat sanctuary much.

Klaus: Whoever showed up was welcome. Once, I looked down and thought there was a new black and white cat brushing up against my leg — then didn't move until the skunk ambled away. We had our moments!

Valerie: I used to love/hate going there as a little kid, bringing food and treats with me. I was happy that I could help them, but hated the idea that they had no home to be warm and cuddled.

Klaus: The cubicles were warmer than most homes, the sanctuary was built on a warm outcrop of the underground part of the Parliament Buildings, and we replaced the straw every fall. In fact, many of the cats slept outside because some of the cubicles were too warm, even in the winter.

Valerie: I knew they were okay when I got older, but when I was very young all my mind saw was no homes, scared and hungry cats. It made me proud when I was little to bring them food and treats. I'd sit quietly for hours watching them.

Klaus: Also remember they were feral and knew how to survive outside, even in the winter. There were many days when it was -20 and I would find them sunning themselves on the deck.

Caroline: I miss this so much. I wish they were still there, and those cats were useful too! Wonder how they keep the rodents under control now? I mean the real ones, not the politicians.

Debbie: Why was it closed in the end?

Ted: Made people think of the fat cats next door, so it had to go?

Klaus: I knew in 2008, when René went into a retirement home, that it was the beginning of the end. We also knew then that it would eventually be demolished for the new tourist centre.

Diana: Another thing taken away by Harper?

Lucy: No, Prime Minister Harper had a special love for cats.

Klaus: Harper loved the colony. When he left Parliament at the end of the day he used to wave and ask me how the cats were doing. In actual fact, the government had nothing to do with the cats. René Chartrand rented the land from the Crown, not the Government, so in effect, it belonged to the Queen.

Barbara: That was a very special place for animals to go to be loved and fed. You, Brian, and René are the best kind of people. I know that René has passed on and I'm sure he's in the best place in heaven.

SECOND WINTER

Last Train to Wakefield

Last train to Wakefield in this winter shot shared by Alexander Poirier, showing three cars from the Swedish train set that eventually took over the run to Wakefield from the Canada Science and Technology Museum CP 1201. Due originally to washouts along the tracks, the Wakefield Steam Train hasn't run since 2011 and, as Alexander observed, it's slowly losing its battle with Mother Nature – and delinquents.

Ian: Oh my, look at that "art."

Jun: The graffiti adds to it.

Paul: And graffiti is very much a part of train culture.

Andy: No, the graffiti is disgusting. Done by vandals and thugs.

Jun: Agree to disagree.

Justin: At least it's good artistic tagging. Ottawa generally lacks in that. Also it's making it a canvas for art vs. slowly eroding scrap.

Paul: They could make it a legal graffiti wall. The end result would be better than simply letting it rot.

Mary: Terrible that someone would deface these cars. On the other hand, it's terrible to have them sit there and not be used. Maybe they should have been parked in Wakefield and used as a restaurant or B&B, therefore still attracting visitors to this beautiful town and its surroundings. Love Wakefield!

Andy: Unfortunately, the equipment was on the Hull side of the washout when it happened.

Roger: Can't they use the trains for tourism, a museum, or even set them together in a casino? Something better than wasting away?

Max: Nothing much historical about the train, unfortunately, since the engine and cars were from Sweden.

Nancy: I recall there was a kitchen. They could have turned it into a great theme restaurant.

Marguerite: They could always be transformed into housing for the homeless.

Marie: How long did this train run?

Lee: This particular tourist train ran for 15 years, but only in the summer.

Lyndsay: So sad. My husband and I took the dinner train when we got married. It was awesome.

Lynn: Loved riding this train to Wakefield and having lunch at the Mill. They had folk singers and we used to sing along with them. Supper at night was fabulous.

Carole: When I lived in Wakefield, it was so nice to hear it and see the train coming into the village.

Paul: Loved watching people turning it around on the turntable in Wakefield.

Wayne: It provided a very scenic trip beside the Gatineau River. They should consider getting it operational again to benefit all concerned.

Toon: Not only a lost tourist opportunity but a lost opportunity to develop a rail network to Chelsea, Wakefield and points along the way. Imagine this train making a regular run, mornings and evenings, ending at Bayview.

Nick: What is needed for this line to get back up and running? When we first moved to Ottawa nearly ten years ago there was talk that it would be up "within a year or two."

Mo: The rail bed collapsed on the hill north of Hull after heavy rain. No one had the millions to repair it.

Alain: Try $50 million-plus to repair and stabilize …

Tim: Not to mention the town of Chelsea ripped up all the tracks in its area.

Max: For use as a bike path.

Rick: The tracks were washed out before they were removed. Sadly, it was determined that the cost to replace them was simply astronomical. No blame goes to Chelsea. They were just cleaning up the mess and trying to repurpose the track bed.

Alexander: Plus, the coaches themselves are in a sorry state and, being from Sweden, the parts would be extremely difficult to come by.

Lee: I'm thinking maybe they should have called it LRT … and got billions!

(Shared by Alexander Poirier)

An Outdoor Rink in Alta Vista

Classic shot of 150 Ottawa kids showing up in January of 1957 at an outdoor rink in Alta Vista for figure-skating lessons with one-time world champion Andrea Bernolak (nee Kékesy).

That's a wee Judy Bonnar on the left and a wee Judy Staples on the right, with Mrs. Bernolak, as she is called in the newspaper article, in the middle.

Caitlin: Very cool. I believe Judy Bonnar lived in our house.

Chris: We lived on Hillary, across from the Bernolaks. She was an interesting, talented lady who kept up her sporting endeavours by kayaking well into her later years.

Leona: I remember an Andrea Bernolak from the 1970s who was with the River Runners. She was known to have perfect balance and never to capsize.

Domenic: Andrea Bernolak still lives in Alta Vista.

Diane: Is this the rink below Alta Vista Public School? The reason I ask is that I grew up on Snowdon Street in the 1950s and '60s and also took skating lessons there on Saturday morning.

Ian: Yes, Alta Vista Public School. I attended in 1955-56, and 1961-63. You can see the old water tower by the fire hall. Later, there was a double rink on the west side of the school, with a hockey rink inside the boards and public skating on the outside.

El: I learned to skate on the rink with the hockey in the middle. God, my feet would get cold!

Rick: The rink in the picture was built on the school grounds to the northeast of the school. The houses on the left fronted on Orillia, and the houses at the top fronted on Alta Vista. I forgot it ever existed.

Liz: I may actually be in this picture. I lived on Orillia street and learned to skate at this rink.

George: I skated on this rink all through the '60s! Wonderful to see it!

Warren: I remember being sent out from gym class to scrape the "north side" rink with the heavy, wide-blade, black-steel shovels. We'd link the shovels side-by-side in groups and plow the rink in two or three passes.

Jennifer: I lived on Heron Road, used to walk through the Evans farm property – through the gravestones! – to the rink at Alta Vista.

Bruce: This was back in the days when parent volunteers would assist in flooding and shovelling and watching the skate hut.

Rebecca: Still do it today!

Gwen: I see my house, but the funny thing is that I don't remember this rink. I only remember the one we skated at most Friday and Saturday nights, the one with the shack. We would go into the shack to warm up. Girls on one side, boys on the other, with the stove in between. You could look into the other side, and if someone of the opposite sex that you were crushing on went back out on ice, you quickly followed. Wonderful memories!

Ian: Girls wore white (figure) skates and boys wore brown or black (hockey) skates. Times have changed since then!

Doug: We skated on a rink like this at the City View Public School on Canter Boulevard in the late 1950s and early 1960s. No wimpy indoor rinks for us!

Ann: Our beautiful rink was in Weston Park, behind our house on Othello in Elmvale Acres. We would head there after supper and stay until they turned out the rink lights around 9 p.m. That cold fresh air ... we were so healthy! Still my favourite go-to park for the memories. First kissed a boy there ... and yes, I liked it!

(City of Ottawa Archives CA042626)

Carlington Ski Hill

Bruce McDonald shares a mute reminder of the glory days of the Carlington Ski Hill, which is the old ski hill you can still see beside the quarry near Carling and the Queensway.

Much used by local skiers after it opened circa 1965, ski operations ended at the close of the 1989-90 season. This year I heard it's being re-purposed for mountain-biking. Can hardly wait to try that in the winter!

Fraser: I believe Carlington was used for skiing much earlier than 1965. I taught beginners there in the late 1950s ... I think!

VR: I remember skiing at Carlington over Christmas in 1967. We used to go there when it was really too cold to drive all the way up to Camp Fortune and spend big bucks just to freeze.

Anne: It was a great place to ski on a school night when you couldn't make it to Fortune and, looking back, we were lucky to have it. Better than hanging around in shopping malls.

Minx: I learned to ski on this hill, which I could walk to. Spent every weekend there for a couple of winters.

(Shared by Bruce McDonald)

Steven: Used to walk there every day after school. Couldn't wait to get volumes of 30-second runs in.

Tasha: A nice little hill, perfect for me. Took night lessons there in the early 1980s. Shame it's gone.

Michael: My friends's dad took us to Carlington for my first ever time on skis! I remember looking down from the top and saying, "I'll never make it down there alive!"

Mike: I remember not so much the hill, but the rope tow. I'd end up crossing my skis, then get dragged along until I finally let go of the rope and pushed off to the side, so other skiers coming up behind wouldn't run over me.

Heather: I hated being dragged up the lift, but the skiing was fun.

Cruise: I remember (being a little dude) that lift would pick us right up off the ground!

Rose: I was too small to use the ski lift and had to go up the hill sideways!

Janet: There was also a treacherous toboggan hill off the side that had several icy lanes. Went airborne a few times there!

Brandon: Dangerously fun! Now fenced off and not maintained.

Michael: I think it was named Four Lanes. Crazy hill!

Michael: Yes, Four Lanes. I saw a (drunk) guy break his leg there one night.

Dan: We called it "Killer Lanes" as kids!

Brandon: Carlington was rated the top toboggan hill in North America very recently.

Terri: We used to ride our bikes down that hill in the summer. No helmets, of course ...

Gary: I don't know how fast we got going – but it would have hurt!

Bill: Rode my bike down that grassy hill once in summer. The grass was wet, the rubber of my brakes and the rubber of the wheels got wet ... stopping was a bit of a problem ... "ditched" at the bottom and survived with very few scrapes. First and last time I did that!

Michael: I knew a guy who rode his bicycle down the ski hill. Wiped out, got the handle bars in the guts, gouged himself open!

Beverley: Good times and great falls were had there!

Jill: It was also a great place to pass a summer evening with a friend and a bottle, with the river in the distance on a clear night, and a wonderful sunset.

Katrina: And of course the "tequila sunrise" on the last day of school.

Linda: Okay, so why was the ski hill shut down?

Jay: Probably because it was fun.

Linda: Ottawa has a habit of doing that!

The Tartan Mobile

January 14, 2018: 287 likes, 43 shares, 34 comments, 22,674 reached

You always wanted one, and here it is — your awesome tartan car parked in front of the Universal Appliances store on Rideau in January of 1957.

Actually, the car was being used to promote Maytag's new "Highlander" washing machine as being extra "thrifty." No Scottish stereotypes there!

Barbara: Great picture! When somebody says they bought from Universal Appliances you know they bought high quality!

Margaret: Universal was then at 409 Rideau Street. It's still going strong out Bank Street.

Lynn: This store was started by my father Maurice Ladouceur, and managed by Ralph Richmond. It relocated to 1915 Bank Street, but is still a family business owned by my mother Rae Ladouceur.

Bev: They certainly had a cool car!

Katherine: Is that really a plaid paint job on the car?

Mary: The Tartan Car!

Andre: I believe it's a Mercury.

Bram: Split windshield suggests a 1952 Mercury or Monarch.

Paul: Love the white walls. They should bring those back.

Ann: What a car — tartan or no! The old-style split windshield reminds me of ladies 'nylons' with the black seams.

Brian: My recollection is that Maytag was high quality, but also quite pricey.

Bradley: They needed lots of money to pay the Maytag Man not to do anything.

Delores: Well worth the purchase price, having only had two washing machines in my adult life. First one lasted over 25 years. The second is still going strong after 30 years with no service calls!

Shirley: We lived on Friel Street, just around the corner, I remember going to Universal with my grandfather when he purchased his first television in the early 1950s.

Barb: Our first TV (circa 1953) was a Motorola.

Max: And look, Universal Appliances sold those.

Francois: I see Imbro's restaurant next to Universal.

Brian: When Imbro's was good.

Ann: And they had incredible pizzas. My then-hubby and I used to laugh and

say, "let's go to Embryos." Yup, we were teenagers.

Delores: At one time, Imbro's was the only place in town that made pizza.

Ann: Even before The Colonnade?

Francois: I think so, because the Colonnade opened sometime in the late 1960s.

Delores: Long before the Colonnade. Their website says they opened in 1967, and I'm talking back in the 1950s and early 1960s. I read that Imbro's first opened in 1922 and claimed to be Ottawa's first Italian restaurant.

Monique: My hubby says the Del Rio on Rideau Street was Ottawa's first pizza place ... early 1960s?

Andre: Dined at Imbros many times in the 1960s. Best spaghetti and meat balls in town.

Paul: I lived at 215 Friel, right around the corner. Next to Imbro's was a synagogue and across the street was Dain's (or Dane's) grocery store.

Francois: I remember there was also a garage where my father used to get the tires on his car changed every spring and fall. Don't remember the name ... moved to Belfast Road.

Danielle: Commercial Tire?

Francois: Yes! Commercial Tire!

Francois: I went to De La Salle Academy and saw that area change a lot, with so many homes torn down to make way for the school track, as well as the "creation" of the new St. Patrick Street. Much of Lower Town's character disappeared — along with many of its inhabitants, expropriated by the city to make way for urban renewal.

Danielle: The worst of times for those whose homes were expropriated, but also for those who stayed.

How Not to Park

January 20, 2018: 259 likes, 40 shares, 40 comments, 20,155 reached

How not to park, as demonstrated by this suburban Ottawa driver in 1957. The original record didn't say where this particular ditch was, but people had a lot of fun trying to identify the neighbourhood. The only problem? Houses like these were built all over town in the 1950s and '60s. Giant ditches, too, they say.

Elayne: If the house in behind was on a corner, I would swear it was my childhood home in Fisher Heights. We had ditches like that as well. It must have been the same builder's project!

Daniel: Ditches like this were quite common to neighbourhoods back in the '50s. Ours in Pine Glen were the same.

Tom: I was thinking the Carleton Heights area, maybe City View, because I remember them ditches ...

Gertrude: We lived in a house on Kilborn in Applewood Acres, west of Alta Vista, for many years. The original owners told us about moving into a completed home, but waiting two years for the roads to be finished. Their first winter, they actually had a ladder to climb up the bank of the ditch to get to their house. Next winter, the level of the road had been raised to the level of the house, but there were still massive ditches. They had to cross wooden planks to get from their unpaved road to their still-unpaved driveways.

Rick: Sure looks like Elmvale Acres. We moved onto Dauphin Road when it was still mud. We also had a couple of wide boards leading from our porch to the street, since our front lawn was also mud.

Les: I agree. Elmvale Acres. My dad told me there were huge ditches there before they put in the trees and I can almost tell you the intersection by the style of the houses. It could be Arch Street near the entrance to the park.

David: Doesn't look like the same style of houses as in Elmvale, given the bathroom window in the front. I grew up on Chapman Boulevard. Thinking more Alta Vista area.

Grant: This looks like a Campeau home in Elmvale Acres or perhaps on Smyth Road.

Gertrude: It's probably a Campeau home, but it's impossible to say where because they were built in pockets all over the city for a period of about seven years.

Steve: These are Campeau builds. Probably from 1955 to 1965 in the Meadowlands/Woodroffe area. More in Alta Vista, Navaho Drive, Maitland etc...

Francois: Actually kind of looks like that area in the east end where the streets are lettered, as in A street, B street, etc. Same type of houses there.

Tom: The houses look military. Possibly Fisher and Carling?

Johanne: I think it's the house at 95 Crownhill at the corner of Dunham in Cardinal Heights. The trees have grown, but I'm certain this is the house.

Norm: Wherever it is, it's a shame about the classic car. It would be worth big bucks today.

William: Looks a lot like my grandpa's 1950 Dodge.

Ray: Angle parking was popular at the time.

Linda: "I'll be a little late this morning."

Bryan: Slow slide into the ditch.

Ann: Like a spoon in a dish of ice cream.

Don: Time to put the snow tires on!

Edith: Did they have snow tires back then?

Cathy: Maybe studded tires.

Richard: Hope he was wearing the non-existent seatbelt ...

Ruthanne: Given the date, it's amazing there isn't a driver-sized hole in the windshield!

Mick: From what I see, nothing's changed in Ottawa?

Michael: It's good to know Ottawa drivers aren't necessarily getting worse.

David: Car's just getting a drink of water.

Mark: I'd say that was a "last ditch effort" at stopping. Worked, too!

Sparks Street Solution

January 27, 2018: 219 likes, 26 shares, 25 comments, 14,478 reached

Everyone seems to agree that Sparks Street needs a revival, so here's a "lost" idea from Sparks Street's first anniversary as a permanent pedestrian mall, an event that took place in 1968, when they put up these outdoor canvasses for Ottawa artists to paint on.

When the artists needed a break, they could repair to the Honey Dew for a coffee or a juice. No Starbucks in those days! I do wonder, however, what happened to their paintings.

Dianne: Love this idea.

Joanne: Very cool! Resurrection is in order!

Susan: Bring it back as part of the new Sparks Street revitalization.

Albert: Send this idea to the mayor's office. Bring it back for the busker festival 2018. You never know, we could have a hidden Picasso out there.

Donna: I like the idea of artists working on Sparks Street like they do in Quebec City. Then you'll need a lot of specialty food shops (bagels, donuts,

(Photo: Maurice Button, shared by Trevor Button)

cupcakes, etc.) and nice little eateries (not chains). A fountain with seating around it. Lots of interactive things to do. Lots of comfortable seating. Lots of plants and trees. Years ago there was a little nut shop and they sold warm nuts. Nice memory.

Raymond: Morrow's Nut House!

Donna: I worked on Elgin Street and used to go to Sparks Street on my lunch break. The warm nuts were such a nice treat.

Glenn: Yum, fresh roasted nuts. Oh, how I miss Morrow's.

Tania: But look, even back then there isn't remotely a crowd looking at this.

Julie: Indeed. Makes me curious. Is there no crowd because it was normal to make art on Sparks back then? Or was this during work hours? Do you need crowds to prove that art-making and animation of public space is worth it? In any case, this idea from a former time on Sparks is just beautiful, and I love how it feels so normal. Like something you'd see in Paris.

Tania: I think pushing Sparks as a creative corridor, flanked with interesting shops or eateries, could revitalize it. Even as a little kid in the early 1980s, I remember it being more vibrant then than it is now.

Julie: Absolutely! I've already sent Sparks Street an e-mail to see what I'd need to do to get some movies and performers on Sparks this summer – let's see what happens. Even just cartoonists and portrait artists are a huge hit in most major cities.

Bill: Paintings would probably get trashed in a matter of hours these days.

Katoo: How long before they are covered in graffiti?

Max: Or stolen.

Liz: We'll have to try and keep you guys out of the area!

Joe: It's still a good idea. I've had a few paintings stolen in my life over the years and, in retrospect, it's flattering!

Susan: I used to take breaks outside there and remember watching these artists paint their masterpieces (while rating the guys who walked by!).

Doreen: I remember this, and very much remember the Honey Dew, too. Our neighbour worked there and my dad worked nearby.

Rosemary: My aunt used to bring me to the Honey Dew. I loved their drinks.

Doreen: I loved their drinks too. I can still almost taste them in my mind.

Kathy: I remember the Honey Dew very well. It was a focal point of Sparks Street and you often went to the mall specifically to get a delicious Honey Dew juice.

Linda: Let's bring back the Honey Dew.

Max: As well as the streetcars!

Karen: Excellent idea!

Neither Sleet, Nor Snow ...

Clarence Heron delivers the mail on Rural Route 4, just outside Ottawa in 1960. No steering-wheel-on-the-wrong-side-of-the-specialized-vehicle for him.

I've always wondered, however, having never really lived in the country, how often the post box got knocked off by the snowplow.

Paul: How often were the mailboxes knocked off? Hardly ever. Plow drivers were considerate people — and in those days we drove constantly on unplowed roads without much worry. Today, people don't know how to drive on dry roads period.

Elizabeth: Grew up on RR2 Cumberland, which is now part of Ottawa. Never remember the mailbox being knocked down. Country roads were not plowed as much or as often as these days.

Jeff: Grew up on a road like that RR1 Wilson's Corners, in Val Des Monts. Our plows were better trained, or more respectful, because we never lost our box!

Anne: Still happens. Our mailbox was hit by the snowplow last Friday. Guess the guy didn't realize I saw him stop and look at it.

James: Probably happens more now than back then.

Tony: Our mail still gets delivered this way and the mailbox gets knocked over quite often!

Marlene: We were on First Line Road outside of Manotick, which was RR1. Mailboxes were usually gone at least once a winter.

Billy: We had our mailbox on Eagleson Road (then a dirt road) knocked over on occasion over the years.

Ian: Eagleson was a horrible road in the mid-to-late '70s when I lived in Glen Cairn. In the spring, you risked your car driving on that washboard.

Billy: In 1971 the snow banks on Eagleson were 18 feet high. Our wing blade couldn't push anything and we had to use a bulldozer.

Laurie: My grandfather's mail route in the 1940s was Eagleson, Hazeldean, Stittsville. My grandmother was postmistress of Stittsville for years.

Gail: The person in this car is my dad on his daily mail round! When I was young I used to go with him. He was the kindest, gentlest person you could ever know. Miss him everyday.

Tom: Was he from the Heron family that had a farm on Heron Road off Alta Vista?

(Library and Archives Canada PA-061726)

Gail: Yes, he sure was.

Sharron: I never knew him personally, but loved hearing stories about him from you and Bob. He seemed like quite the character!

Bob: I have great memories of my Uncle Clarence. He always scared me ... in a good way.

Gail: Bob is so right! He used to scare the pants off of us. Then he would go away laughing. It was never in a bad way, always meant in fun. Kind and gentle soul.

Timothy: Your dad (and possibly you) would have delivered mail to our family farm, which was on Hawthorne Road then. NCC expropriated it for the Greenbelt at the end of that year.

Gail: My dad did deliver mail on Hawthorne, but I never made it that far on his route — all that stopping and starting usually made me car sick!

Donna: Where is RR4?

Glenn: Old Highway 31, now Bank Street from Albion Road to Leitrim Road.

Gail: RR4 was south of the city at that time and his route was all the way to Manotick, down to Edwards and back into the city via Conroy. When he retired they split his route between three mailmen — *and* he was a full time dairy farmer!

Black Sabbath

Here's an ad for a rock concert at the Civic Centre in July of 1971, featuring headliner Black Sabbath, with Alice Cooper and the English group Yes as the warm-up bands.

I was at this concert. Most of us had never heard of Yes and were absolutely amazed by them. Alice Cooper, then of biting-the-heads-off-chickens fame, was mightily entertaining. Black Sabbath was terrible. After a few tunes from them, most people walked out.

(Shared by Adam Fonzarelli)

Eric: I was at that show and actually went to see Yes! Their third album was out – the Yes Album.

John: Yes was a revelation. Alice Cooper was weird and intriguing. Sabbath couldn't hold my scattered attention after that.

Mike: Alice Cooper was GREAT. His song "I'm Eighteen" had just come out. I had just turned 18 two days before the concert, and the drinking age in Ontario had just dropped to 18. Great summer!

Bob: Sabbath was booed, as I recall.

Robert: I really wanted to see Black Sabbath, but Alice Cooper and Yes blew them off the stage. I was probably one of the ones booing Black Sabbath. One of the worst bands I ever saw.

David: Went to see Sabbath, but Yes stole the show. Rick Wakeman was the real star. Alice was good. Sabbath, as I remember it, was just very loud.

Bob: Rick Wakeman of Yes was worth five dollars all by himself.

Enrique: Wasn't Tony Kaye the keyboardist for Yes on that tour?

Sean: If you go to a Black Sabbath show and leave talking about the keyboard player of Yes, something went seriously wrong, haha!

Mike: Yes was by far the best of the night. Sabbath, I still blame for my ear damage. Of course, it was my decision to stand so close to the towers … in my, ah, somewhat altered state.

Thomas: Ear damage close to the towers? I was way up in the stands and heard nothing but ringing for three days.

Mike: I'm still hearing it!

Tom: I arrived late … but, wow, what a concert at an amazing price. Three bands for mere pennies.

Anna: I was there. It was my first concert and it was FABULOUS. About a year later Alice Cooper returned with his next show "Dead Babies," in which Alice either hanged himself or had his head chopped off with a guillotine. Wild even now!

Steve: According to an article in the January 1982 edition of CKCU's Trans FM magazine (is that still around?), the original concert was supposed to co-headline Iggy and the Stooges and Alice Cooper, but that show was cancelled, and I quote, "… when Iggy stabbed himself with a drumstick. Co-headliner Cooper was rescheduled with Yes and Black Sabbath for a concert that is still remembered by early metal fans … and the Civic Centre security people who scraped the whisky bottles and vomit off the floor for weeks." So there you go. History!

Jack: Yes came back in 1972 with the J. Geils Band. Half the people went to see Yes and half went to see J. Geils. Everyone left happy.

Tara: This Sabbath concert would have been kick-ass! Too bad I wasn't born yet!

Mickey: I was at that concert. I even remember some of it …

Patti: I *seem* to recall being there …

Norm: I attended this concert and — from what I remember — the acid was something else!

David: Sold more LSD that night then ever. Wish I had more!

Larry: Yes knocked my socks off. They're still in the Civic Centre somewhere. Size 10.

The Old Spaghetti Factory

The entrance to The Old Spaghetti Factory, located on York Street, just east of Dalhousie in the Byward Market. Shown here in 1979, four years after it opened, the restaurant went bankrupt in 1986. That might seem pretty fast for a popular restaurant but, if there's one thing we learn in Lost Ottawa, it's that the lifetime of most restaurants is remarkably brief.

Zachary: Maybe it would still be open if they sold new spaghetti?

Max: Oh, man ...

Zachary: Somebody had to say it.

Janey: I used to love going to the Spaghetti Factory. That loaf of warm bread they gave you while waiting for dinner ... yum!

David: Best dish ever was their spaghetti with browned butter and mizithra cheese.

Neil: Burnt butter and mizithra cheese is all I ever ordered.

Francyne: It's the only thing I ever ordered. I think I was addicted to it!

Janice: Best deal for the undecided was to order spaghetti pasta with a choice of four sauces, one scoop on each quarter of the plate.

Claude: I seem to recall the placemats had this story of how spaghetti grew on trees.

Kevin: I still have the puzzle of a plate of spaghetti with sauce they sold as a novelty.

Tim: The Spaghetti Factory was a great place for a teenager to get a relatively cheap meal. Remember the old trolley car inside with the preferred seating?

Brenda: I remember having dinner in the trolley with high-school friends. Loved that place!

Pat: It was great. They didn't check ID.

Andrew: I worked here as a busboy when I was 15. By the time I was 16, I was already a bartender. Yes, that was illegal. I can still taste the meat sauce...

Denise: I worked there, learning how to carry two large trays at the same time, one with drinks and the other with food.

Andrew: And it was insane when two of those trays hit the floor at the same time!

Elaine: I remember this restaurant so well. Going with grandma and grandpa. The time Sarah Canuck fell asleep in a plate of spaghetti ...

Melissa: Went there on a date with my first boyfriend when I was 16.

Elizabeth: I only ever went there one time. Both my date and I ended up with food poisoning, so nothing but bad memories for me!

Laurie: Went with three friends and got a huge big piece of glass in my mouth. They were very upset. I guess something got broken.

Roger: I think there was also a bar called Brandy's next door around that time.

Sylvie: Brandy's was the in-place to go with your girlfriends if you were single!

Andrew: Brandy's was a meat market, as I recall.

Elayne: Brandy's was great.

Stephen: I was a DJ at Brandy's and then later on the fifth floor. Long, strange trip ...

Jack: Anyone hang at the nightclub in the back called Scotland Yard?

Denise: The Yard was a good place to have a brew after work.

Wendy: What's in that building now?

Dave: The Whiskey Bar has been in there for 15 years. It was called Hoolihan's before that.

Richard: Ah, yes Hoolihan's.

Monique: Not sure what's there now but Lips Bar was the place to be in the late 1980s or so.

Nancy: One of my first trips to downtown Ottawa with girlfriends was for a dinner out at the Old Spaghetti Factory. You got to keep your glass.

Roger: I remember they had two drinks. One called "The Conductor," and the other called "Jump up and Kiss Me." Had both glasses at home.

Jocelyn: I still have two Conductor glasses!

Cindy: I got engaged at the Spaghetti Factory. Still have the glasses. Not the husband.

(Carleton Resolution, 1980-81)

Drinks at the Claude

One of Ottawa's many fine drinking establishments, here's the Claude Hotel on the southwest corner of Beechwood and Loyer Street in 1987. Despite its remarkable exterior, it was knocked down to make a parking lot for what is now the Metro supermarket. I'm sure all those people with mansions in Rockcliffe were deeply saddened!

Leona: Ah, yes! Ontario liquor-licensing laws of old that didn't allow windows. You wouldn't want anyone walking by to see people inside enjoying an adult beverage.

Peter: I used to tipple a bit there myself in the 1970s. Small plastic or white enamel-topped tables, the old wooden chairs, granite floors, surly waiters and not much ambience. Men-only on one side, Ladies and Escorts on other.

Robin: It was the haunt of many an underage Ashbury student. They never asked for ID ... unless they were forewarned a bust was coming. Remember the quarts well.

John: Neon lighting that buzzed, quarts of beer costing a dime more on the Ladies and Escorts side, What's not to like?

Palmer: Drinking games with those small seven-ounce draft glasses that were still 25 cents each in 1978. C'mon, drink up!

Maurice: I lived on Alice Street in early the 1980s and stopped in after work most every night. Very entertaining I must say!

Andre: A drinkin', playin' pool and smokin' kind of place.

Elizabeth: That's where my dad drank.

Carole: Both my grandfathers drank there. Grandfather Demers lived across the street.

Pete: Used to go there all the time. Great spot.

Chris: Great jukebox too!

Jason: Looks like a great place ... to get stabbed.

Russell: I recall it had a reputation for being rough.

Yvon: Got in my very first bar fight the very first night I went in there.

Gord: It was a dump ...

Bill: Those "dumps" were usually among the best drinking spots, but in my early days I soon learned to sit with my back against the wall facing the door in the "lounge" and the men's washroom.

Nick: I went in there once with a friend in the mid-1980s after an afternoon funeral. We were both wearing suits. Based on the looks we got and what I heard from the other patrons, it was the only time in my life I thought I'd get queer-bashed. Finished our beer really quick, got the hell out.

Steve: A friend and I planned to go there for a drink on the Claude's last night in 1990. It would have been my one and only visit, but as we approached the place we were told that there was a police drug raid underway and it was therefore closed. Maybe it's just as well that I never got to see the inside!

Robert: The mayor of Vanier at the time was Gisèle Lalonde who vowed to clean up Vanier — and poof! Three bars disappeared in a very short period of time, including the Claude, Maple Leaf and Lafontaine.

Mike: The Lafontaine burned down.

Pierre: The Maple Leaf burned down, too, if I'm not mistaken.

Robert: Yes it did, but it was probably an "accident!"

Daniel: I think there was a grocery store behind the Claude that used to be an IGA belonging to the Joanisse family?

Denis: Yes, and I worked at the IGA packing groceries. The husbands would park their cars and go for a pint (or eight) while their wives did the grocery shopping. I'd carry the groceries to the car and load the trunk. Guys who had a few brews under their belts always tipped the best!

Pierre: You'd load up the car ... while the bartender loaded up the husband.

(City of Ottawa Archives CA024445)

149

Scotts Chicken Villa

Friday Night in Lost Ottawa in 1992, when you could still grab a quick dinner at the Scott's Chicken Villa on the corner of Dalhousie and St. Andrew. Alas, the Colonel left the building some time ago, so maybe it wasn't so finger lickin' good after all?

I remember getting Kentucky Fried Chicken only once in my entire childhood. With seven kids in the family, I can imagine why! And KFC never did learn how to make good French fries.

Vince: Back in the 1960s and '70s the fries were terrible, but the chicken and gravy were quite good.

Paul: Terrible fries, so years ago we would pick up some chicken and then get fries at a chip wagon.

Matt: The KFC fries were horrible. Soggy, white and lacking salt. They bent when you tried to dunk 'em in gravy! Best fries were at Harvey's.

Steve: My parents liked KFC when we lived in Bells Corners in the early 1970s. Fries tasted much the same as the box.

Sophie: Ah, the good old days! For some reason the Colonel's hot buttery bread comes to mind.

(City of Ottawa Archives CA024508)

Timothy: My dad would bring home the family barrel with that mystery gravy and "Grecian" (what!?) bread.

Peter: The "Grecian" bread always made me snicker. About as far away from proper European bread as one could get.

Alex: Don't forget the neon green coleslaw.

Bryan: Hey, I loved that green coleslaw!

Deborah: I was going to say ... I liked the coleslaw.

Carole: I worked at this particular KFC for many years, but St. Laurent was known for having the best KFC in town.

Marilyn: In the 1960s my dad would head to the KFC on St. Laurent every Friday night. He loved that greasy stuff.

Denis: My dad used to get KFC whenever his kids had a birthday. Then he discovered the Red Barn, where the chicken was way better and cost less. We went there instead until Red Barn closed.

Dave: Back in the 1960s, my mom would send my sister and I to pick up a family meal. We would sneak a few fries each on the way home. Eventually we graduated to a piece of chicken each. Needless to say that was one less piece each at supper.

Andy: Minor hockey used to get Kentucky Fried Chicken for their end-of-year banquets in the 1980s. My parents were not impressed, but my brother and I were happy!

Sergio: In our youth, we would stop at KFC to get buckets for our family picnics at Lac Philippe — then compete with the chipmunks trying to steal our food!

Sylvie: I'm having memories of my mom joining me for lunch and eating in the car when I worked on Dalhousie. It was not as greasy as today's KFC.

Bob: You just need something to wash down all that oil on the chicken. A cold glass of milk does the trick ...

Tobin: One of my best friends lived at 106 St. Andrew and worked at the KFC on Dalhousie, which was maybe 100 yards from his family home. He always made sure to finish his closing shift with lots of leftovers for us. R.I.P., Marc Carriere!

Denise: OMG, I use to live across the street from this KFC. That's all I could smell every night!

Rick: I lived up the street on St. Andrew but must not have visited often enough ... it closed when I lived there.

Dave: I'll never forget the woman's face when I walked into this particular KFC one night looking for poutine and mistakenly asking for a "putain." Oops! It turns out pronunciation is quite important ...

The Phoenix and the Rat

How about a Lost Ottawa matinee at the Phoenix Theatre? Here's the cinema in 1991, when it was still located 415 Bank Street, across from Florence Street.

The Phoenix favoured arty foreign films and rose from the ashes of what was previously the Rialto — the "Rat Hole"— which had sadly passed through its kung fu and porn movie phases. Currently, the site is a very fine parking lot.

Blair: The Rialto opened in 1943, so it had a pretty long run before it became the Phoenix. The building was over 50 years old when they tore it down. TV and DVDs took away the audiences of these old cinemas, unfortunately.

Mark: The Phoenix was managed by Frank Taylor, had the first woman projectionist in Ottawa (Stephanie Duncan), and was largely staffed by film studies students from Carleton University. It was a real cinephile's paradise, and is much missed.

Ann: Loved the Phoenix because it played films that never showed up anywhere else in town. I also remember how fast they knocked it down once it closed. Within days, I recall. Like they were trying to avoid any move to save the building.

Bill: The first movie to play the Phoenix was the French film *Maleville*. A Rialto hold-over came up to the box office and said "One for Male Evil, please."

Terry: In the early 1970s the Sunday matinee at the Rialto was one dollar and you got three so-so movies.

Barry: I loved that you could see three movies of the same genre at one time: three sci-fi, three westerns, three comedies, etc. I also seem to remember that they had the best hot dogs.

Ken: I remember the Rialto had a hot dog cooker going round and round in the window. The wieners looked like they had been on there for years!

Joseph: Three movies for a quarter in my day. No deals like that anymore, ha!

Lynne: For 35 cents, all-day Elvis movies!

Karen: Three Elvis movies for 50 cents in the late 1960s.

Carole: Passed many Saturday afternoons at the Rialto: Tarzan, Roy Rogers/ Dale Evans and many other westerns, two or three in one afternoon.

Bent: Three Stooges, Hercules.

Elly: Saw my first Spaghetti Westerns at the Rialto, still love Clint and

Charlie! Cheap food, sticky floors, but fun.

Barbara: Spent our allowance on Saturdays there. The floor *was* sticky!

Carl: I remember us going in during the day and coming out in the dark after three movies. Usually kicking the hell out of each other after watching six hours of kung fu movies!

Tom: Went to see many movies there during school ... skipping class to learn martial arts!

Rick: The Bruce Lee triple feature was the best!

Daniel: Dad used to bring me to see kung fu movies. Hot dog, box of popcorn, and an ice cream sandwich.

Eleanor: The Rialto reportedly had fleas so my mother would never let me go there. The Capitol or nowhere!

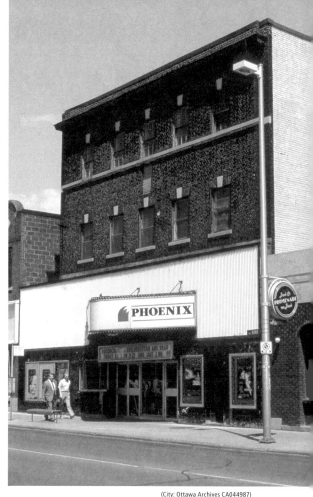

(City: Ottawa Archives CA044987)

Mike: I remember some of the Rialto's seats had no backs or arms or cushions at one time. Careful where you sat!

Carl: Remember the scuzzy, scary bathroom downstairs? Always some weirdos down there. Good times!

Fred: Going to the washroom was like descending into Hell. Great popcorn, though. Maple Leaf chips and RC Cola.

Philip: It was a dump, but we didn't care.

Donald: Used to go to the Rialto every Saturday when I was a kid, and we always called it the Rat Hole.

Wendy: Rat Hole. Yup. That's what we called it. We old!

Daniel: A high school friend used to say the Rat Hole's slogan was "Kill a rat ... get your money back!"

Brian: We called it the Rat Hole ... but that doesn't mean we didn't like it!

Camp Fortune

Here's Camp Fortune in 1960, when the ski hill was still run by the Ottawa Ski Club. How did it get the name Camp Fortune, you ask? Because the ski resort started in the 1920s with the purchase of Garrett Fortune's woodsman's shack at Fortune Hill, next door to Fortune Lake

Un-fortunately, my dad took me there a few times so I could learn how to fall down those hills. He was too cheap to pay for lessons!

Dave: Garret Fortune's property was at the top of the hill. The Dunlop property was at the bottom. Hence the name of Dunlop Road leading into Fortune. I am a sixth generation descendant of Gabriel Dunlop. There is also the Dunlop Picnic Field — at one time it was known as the Garden of Eat-in'.

Thomas: It was at Camp Fortune in the winter of 1960-61 that I started to ski. My dad would give me two dollars, one for the pass, and one for lunch, and I

(Library and Archives Canada 4949936)

always came home with fifteen cents change.

Nini: I learned to ski downhill and cross-country here, both in the same pair of leather boots and skis. For cross-country, I just loosened my boot attachment at the back (rolled wire), and kept the boot toe in its metal side clips and under a leather strap. Sounds really old school, and it was. We spent every Saturday there. One day my sister jumped off the ski jump while we were eating lunch, yelling, "Bombs Away!" She landed not far away from us with only one broken ankle. Not bad for a first jump!

Ted: I learned to ski-jump there. Never turned, just jumped for five years. Then one day I went down the slalom hill with my jumping skis on. Wasn't afraid to catch air on the moguls, jumped with Pat Morris and the Fripp boys, and life was good. Now, I have no knees and I know why!

Tom: I learned to ski there and ended up in the Sacred Heart Hospital.

John: Same here!

Mike: You survived the Sacred Heart Hospital!

John: Hence my choice to play music ...

Frank: It was the Civic for me. I couldn't decide which side of a tree to go around hence ... BANG! Blood everywhere and I still have a good chin scar. I'm laughing now, but ...

Max: Spent many winters ski-jumping off the 60-metre Lockeberg ski-jump beside the slalom hill and rope tow.

Jeff: You jumped that? You're my hero, man! Balls of steel!

Max: I had a lot of practice ... being on the Canadian National ski-jumping team.

Vinson: I loved Camp Fortune. It was the best place to meet people, an Ottawa "melting pot," where you made friends from all over the city.

Madeleine: I went up the t-bar on the slalom hill one Sunday in 1972 with Pierre Elliot Trudeau. We used to see him there regularly.

Lynn: My brother was knocked down while skiing by Pierre Trudeau. Later, in the parking lot, he recognized my brother and came over to apologize again.

Curtis: I worked at Camp Fortune for three winters when the Ottawa Ski Club was at its peak. The largest membership (10,000 people) ski club in the world. One busy place on the weekends when the weather was good.

Don: I thought it was the greatest skiing in the world (until we moved west). Close and fun. On good days, my skis could always be seen on my car in the Hillcrest High parking lot ... until noon.

Camp Fortune: Thanks for posting this one, *Lost Ottawa*! Let us know if you want to perfect that technique your father taught you.

Bill's Joke Shop

Here's that ancient Ottawa institution known as Bill's Joke Shop near the corner of Bank and Nepean. If you were ever shocked, doused with itching powder, or sat on a classic whoopee cushion, chances are it came from Bill's — the source of thousands and thousands of pranks over the years. Now closed, unfortunately.

Paula: This was my family's store for 50 years, started by my grandfather Bill who passed it on to my dad Brian Abrams! The corner of Bank and Nepean! Great childhood memories!

Richard: I hope you realize how much your grandfather's store meant to so many of us ... my brothers and I still talk about it. Cheers!

Morey: I loved Bill's as a kid! It really was an Ottawa institution.

Andrew: Please pass on my best to your dad for his birthday, Paula. Bill's Joke Shop for life!

Gregg: Thanks to you and your family! So many great times! Amazing memories. An iconic Ottawa "place!"

Robert: After moving to Ottawa in 1981, I had no logical reason for going into this store and yet I would find myself wandering in "just to look around," but maybe more, I now think, out of recognition that this was a dying breed of shop and I wanted to be able to remember what these kind of places were like. I may have bought the odd thing here and there, but I mostly just tried to take it all in. Shops like Bill's were something special.

Paula: Such kind and true words Robert. It was the toughest thing for my dad when he had to close. He loved that store so much!

Francois: Saturdays was a ritual for me. Take the #2 bus from the east end, walk down Bank Street and go to Bill's. Whoopee cushions, pepper gum, plastic ice cubes with flies in them ...

Frank: Snapping gum, joy buzzers, kazoos, shell game, squirting flowers, marked cards. The itching powder was industrial grade. Very nasty.

Charlotte: I bought itching powder there ... and yes he had it coming!

Rob: Disappearing ink, rubber poo. You walked in but never left empty-handed. He had all the old favourites and got new stuff all the time.

Paula: My dad and my grandfather loved showing off all of the gags, and I did too as a kid when I would help him out on Saturdays! Wonderful memories!

Jeanne: Purchased one of those pens that you click and it gives you a good shock all the way up your arm. Still have it somewhere.

Peter: Bought my first fake vomit there.

Fred: I wanted the fake vomit so bad ... but was afraid to even touch it.

Jennifer: Whoopee cushions for everyone!

Mike: Whoopee cushions never get old!

Alan: I remember the nickel nailed to the floor so you could never pick it up! Loved that place!

Omar: I remember the liquid smoke and garlic bubble gum. Good times had by all!

Dominique: Bought my fart machine there...

Richard: I bought sneezing powder there.

Vern: And you haven't stopped sneezing since then.

Richard: So that's why!

Glenn: Memories from a more innocent time.

Derek: God, I loved that place as a kid. I remember one time when I was nine and there was a lady in the store who was buying a dildo. The woman at the cash was explaining to the lady how important it was to keep it clean. I was so puzzled as to what a dildo was. I thought it had something to do with magic ...

When the Train Left the Station ...

Everybody knows Union Station, situated downtown across from the Chateau Laurier. The building itself is still lovely, but the old railway infrastructure that used to surround it was interesting, too — particularly the way the Canadian Pacific tracks used to pass along the side of the canal and under Confederation Square, on their way to the Alexandra Interprovincial Bridge.

Here's CP Locomotive 424 departing the station for a trip over the bridge and up the Ottawa Valley to Waltham, Quebec, in June of 1956.

Morgan V: Wow, Waltham makes a picture caption!

Morgan F: Big city stuff!!

Mark: Waltham? That's God's country out there.

Lysanne: I wonder who from Waltham is on board?

Lynne: My dad is leaving for Waltham on that coal-driven train.

Denise: Chances are my dad Paul Charron was the conductor on that train. My family traveled that route many times. I remember so vividly the beautiful and elegant dining car!

Tim: I wonder if I met this train at Waltham when my aunt came to visit my grandfather's farm in Chichester. Uncle Francis would drive his 1951 Chevy over to pick her up.

Gail: The engineer might have been my father!

Rick: Could have been my dad or his dad ... both CPR out of Ottawa West.

Cheryl: My granddad Albert Roud was also an engineer for CPR. I would often stand on this bridge and wave to him as he came in or left the station. Could be him, too. What wonderful memories this picture has brought back to me.

Mike: As a kid living in Old Chelsea during the 1950s, I remember taking the train to Union Station and back. It was an exciting trip, especially going over the Interprovincial Bridge!

Peter: I remember taking the stainless steel Budd-liner from this station many times, up through Gatineau and Wakefield to Messines and Blue Sea Lake. I also remember the steam trains my family would ride from Ottawa to Montreal for shopping.

Alan: I travelled a number of times from the station to Montreal when I was young, and I was in the Chateau Laurier many times when the steam

(Photo: W.C. Whittaker, F.D. Shaw Collection. Shared by Bruce Chapman and Colin Churcher)

locomotives rumbled underneath. I often saw engines reversed on the turntable behind Union Station. Amazing how far we've come!

Judi: I was so fortunate to have my O'Brien grandparents in Montreal and my Murphy grandfather as an engineer. Since his run was to Montreal, I too got to experience those beautiful dining cars. My brother and I were very young, but the conductor would watch out for us. Great memories.

Claire: My friends and I used to take the five p.m. train to Montreal nearly every weekend during the summer, riding the streetcar to the station. Once the station moved ... we stopped taking the train.

Rosemary: One particular memory I have is meeting my boyfriend from Montreal as he arrived on that train. We agreed to meet at the door of the station. The only problem was that I was waiting at the front door on Rideau while he was waiting at the side. There were no cell phones then to call and say, "where the heck are you?"

Dolores: Every time you show us pictures of the trains and the train station it brings me back to 1944-46 when my aunt would take me to Montreal for the summer! I love riding the trains still. My dream was always to go to Vancouver on the train with my five grandchildren ...

Susan: My grandmother told me how she went to meet my grandfather at that station when he returned from the war after being away for five years. Now I can visualize it.

Sherri: When I see these pictures, I imagine how exciting it must have been to be in Canada at this time, particularly for my grandparents who immigrated from Jolly Old England.

Daniel: Visiting Union Station was synonymous with the arrival and departure of my grandparents. I caught a glimpse of what was likely one of the last operating steamers on that very inside track.

Ken: I remember my mother bringing me to see Santa arrive there, circa 1961.

David: My grandfather took me on the train to Ottawa back then, so I remember the old station and also walking underground to the Chateau Laurier.

Rosemary: The tunnel from the Chateau was a nice warm way to get across the street in winter.

Beverly: My friends and I went through that tunnel often after visiting the Parliament Buildings just about every Sunday afternoon.

Lorelei: I remember the old station, the tunnel, and my mom taking me swimming at the Chateau Laurier. Sometimes we would go to the lower level of Freiman's on Rideau Street and get that really yummy chocolate malt in the tulip-shaped glass.

Mark: I never knew what the store was called, I always just knew there was a malt waiting for me at the end of the tunnel. Damn, now I want a malt and it's only eight a.m. in the morning.

Crystal: Love this picture! Each time I see these old train photos from downtown Ottawa, I get the urge to go for a walk and explore where their ghosts pass.

Charles: These train pictures make my day because, from about 1949 to 1954, when I was a very young lad, I would sit on the Driveway with my grandfather and his brother and watch the trains across the canal as they entered the station. My grandfather and his brother always dressed in straw hats, canes in hand, whistling tunes as they walked over to the canal where they would pull out their pocket watches and check times as the trains arrived. What a classy and much-loved generation these gentlemen represented! They knew the schedules, and they knew their railway history – and they were not impressed if a diesel locomotive pulled a train in.

William: Charles, you're so very old of course you would remember scenes like this – but then, so am I, and I even remember the streetcars. I think I have to go and take a nap now ...

Don: This is such a great picture, but do you think any of these trains ever derailed into the canal?

Ian: I'm sure there would be a picture of it on Lost Ottawa if it happened!

About the Author

David McGee's family moved to Ottawa from Victoria, British Columbia in 1966. He attended Graham Park Public, Bayshore Junior High, Greenbank Junior High, and then Sir Robert Borden High School, where he already displayed his love of history. Graduating with a BA in History from Carleton University, he earned a Ph.D. in the History of Science and Technology from the University of Toronto in 1995, then went off to become a post-doctoral Research Fellow, and later Librarian and Archivist at the Dibner Institute for the History of Science and Technology, located at the Massachusetts Institute of Technology in Cambridge, Massachusetts. McGee returned to Ottawa in 2008 to serve as Librarian and Archivist for the  Canada Science and Technology Museum. There, his role in the acquisition of archival material, particularly the Domtar Eddy Booth Collection, brought him into closer and closer connection with the history of the city. He started Lost Ottawa on Facebook in February of 2013.